SCHOLASTIC

Now I Know My

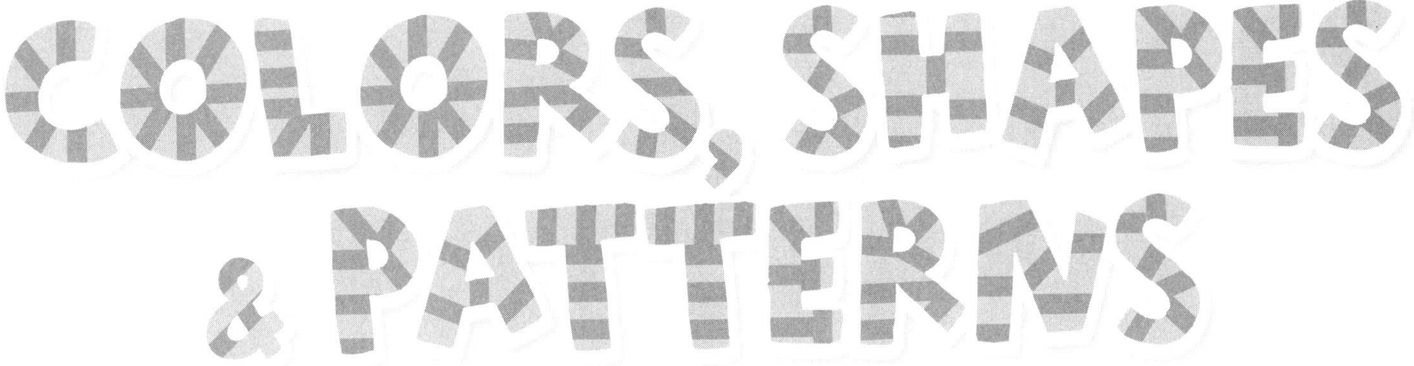

Learning Mats

50+ Double-Sided Activity Sheets That Help Children Learn Key Early Concepts

Lucia Kemp Henry

New York • Toronto • London • Auckland • Sydney
Mexico City • New Delhi • Hong Kong • Buenos Aires

Teaching Resources

Edited by Immacula A. Rhodes
Cover design by Scott Davis
Interior illustrations by Lucia Kemp Henry
Interior design by Holly Grundon

ISBN: 978-0-545-39697-4

Published by Scholastic Inc.
Printed in the U.S.A.

1 2 3 4 5 6 7 8 9 10 40 19 18 17 16 15 14 13 12

Contents

Learning Mats

Colors

Shapes

Learning Mats (continued)

Mat	Skill
45–46.	Oval *(draw and identify ovals; read and write* oval*)*
47–48.	Octagon *(draw and identify octagons; read and write* octagon*)*
49–50.	Star *(draw and identify stars; read and write* star*)*
51–52.	Diamond *(draw and identify diamonds; read and write* diamond*)*
53–54.	Review *(oval, octagon, star, and diamond)*
55–56.	Shape Patterns: AB
57–58.	Shape Patterns: AB
59–60.	Shape patterns: AAB
61–62.	Shape Patterns: ABB
63–64.	Shape Patterns AABB
65–66.	Shape Patterns: ABC
67–68.	Attributes: Color & Shape
69–70.	Attributes: Color & Size
71–72.	Attributes: Shape & Size

Patterns

Mat	Skill
73–74.	Pictures *(mixed patterns)*
75–76.	Pictures *(mixed patterns)*
77–78.	Letters *(mixed patterns; uppercase letters)*
79–80.	Letters *(mixed patterns; uppercase letters)*
81–82.	Letters *(mixed patterns; lowercase letters)*
83–84.	Letters *(mixed patterns; lowercase letters)*
85–86.	Letters *(mixed patterns; mixed letters)*
87–88.	Numbers *(mixed patterns; numbers 1–5)*
89–90.	Numbers *(mixed patterns; numbers 1–9)*
91–92.	Review *(mixed patterns; letters and numbers)*
93–94.	Review *(mixed patterns; pictures and shapes)*
95–96.	Identifying Patterns *(AB)*
97–98.	Identifying Patterns *(AAB)*
99–100.	Identifying Patterns *(ABB)*
101–102. . . .	Identifying Patterns *(AABB)*
103–104. . . .	Identifying Patterns *(ABC)*

About This Book

Welcome to *Now I Know My Colors, Shapes & Patterns Learning Mats*! The 104 double-sided mats in this book provide engaging activities designed to help children master essential early skills and concepts. In addition, the systematic format reinforces literacy and fine-motor skills while enabling children to work independently.

The interactive, reproducible mats feature appealing art and simple, predictable text that targets specific colors, shapes, and patterns. Activities include identifying eight different colors and shapes; reading and writing color and shape words; tracing, drawing, and matching shapes; and recognizing and creating basic patterns with colors, shapes, and symbols. The drawing and writing exercises help develop and strengthen fine-motor skills as well as reinforce shape, letter, and word recognition. And, as children read and follow directions to complete each mat, they build critical vocabulary and comprehension skills. To help meet the learning needs of your students, refer to page 8 to see how activities in this book connect to the Common Core State Standards for Reading (Foundational Skills), Language, and Mathematics, as well as to the standards recommended by the National Council of Teachers of Mathematics (NCTM).

Preparing and using the learning mats is quick and easy! Simply make double-sided copies to use for instruction with the whole class, small groups, student pairs, or individuals. The mats are also ideal for independent work, centers, and homework. You'll find that daily practice with these activities helps build and reinforce knowledge of basic concepts and boosts early literacy skills. Best of all, children will experience the joy of learning as they develop skills that help them grow into more confident, fluent readers.

What's Inside

The learning mats in this resource are divided into three sections: Colors (mats 1–34), Shapes (mats 35–72), and Patterns (mats 73–104). Activities on each mat target a specific color, shape, or pattern. Review mats are also included to provide extra practice for each concept. Although a separate section is dedicated to patterns, activities that involve patterning with colors and shapes are found in those respective sections. Mats in the patterns section give children practice in recognizing, extending, and creating patterns with pictures and symbols (such as letters and numbers).

The mats are ready to use. Simply decide on the skill or topic you want to teach, locate the corresponding mats in the book, and make a double-sided copy of those mats. The only materials kids need for the activities are crayons or colored pencils. To use, children read and follow the directions to complete each activity. You'll find several activity formats throughout the book, as described on pages 6–7.

Colors

- ✤ **Trace and Write:** Children trace the target color word and then write the word on their own without guides. This exercise reinforces letter formation, word recognition, and spelling.
- ✤ **Identify Object Colors:** This activity lets children identify and color objects that are commonly found—in real life—in a specific color.
- ✤ **Identify the Word:** Children use visual discrimination skills to identify the target word from similarly spelled or shaped words.
- ✤ **Drawing:** This activity helps develop fine-motor skills while reinforcing the targeted color concept.
- ✤ **Fill-in-the-Blank:** Children use context by writing the target word in a sentence that connects to the art they drew in the previous activity.
- ✤ **Review:** Color-coded pictures help reinforce color word recognition and fine-motor skills. A writing activity offers additional practice in recognizing, spelling, and writing color words.
- ✤ **Color Patterns:** Children use a color key to create AB, AAB, ABB, AABB, and ABC patterns.

Shapes

- ✤ **Trace the Shape:** To develop shape recognition and fine-motor skills, children trace the target shape in two activities on these mats.
- ✤ **Identify the Shape:** Children identify the target shape from a variety of shapes and then color the appropriate ones.
- ✤ **Trace and Write:** In this activity, children trace the target shape word and then write the word on their own.
- ✤ **Drawing:** To target shape concepts and fine-motor skills, children draw a picture using a specific shape.
- ✤ **Review:** These color-coded pictures reinforce shape word recognition and fine-motor skills. A writing activity gives children more practice in recognizing, spelling, and writing shape words.
- ✤ **Shape Patterns:** Children draw shapes to complete AB, AAB, ABB, AABB, and ABC patterns.
- ✤ **Identify Attributes:** Activities on these mats help sharpen reasoning skills. Children color the shapes and then identify which shape matches the specific attributes stated in the directions.

Patterns

- **Complete the Patterns:** Children complete patterns by drawing pictures or filling in the missing letter or numbers. Each mat features a variety of patterns.
- **Review:** In these activities, children demonstrate understanding of patterns by identifying the item or shape that comes next in a pattern, as well as creating their own patterns.
- **Identify Patterns:** Children identify, label, and create their own AB, AAB, ABB, AABB, and ABC patterns.

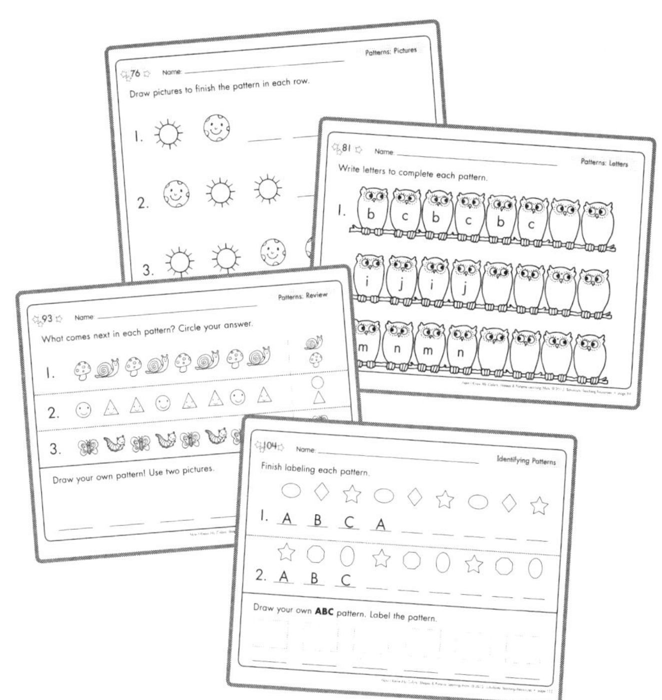

Helpful Tips

The following suggestions will help you and your students get the most out of the learning mats:

- Complete each mat in advance to become familiar with the directions, art, and response for each activity. If desired, laminate your completed copy to use as an answer key. (Or slip the mat into a clear, plastic page protector.) You might bind all of your answer keys into a notebook to keep on hand for children to check their work.
- Use the mats to introduce new concepts, track children's progress in mastering essential skills, and review concepts already covered.
- Prepare the mats for repeated use in learning centers. Simply laminate the double-sided mats and put them in a center along with wipe-off color crayons and paper towels (to use as erasers).
- Compile sets of the learning mats into booklets for children to complete in class or at home. For example, you might staple copies of mats 1–6 between two sheets of construction paper and title the booklet, "My Red, Yellow, and Blue Book."
- The mats are also perfect for instant homework assignments. Send the pages home with children to complete. This is an easy way to reinforce skills covered in class, as well as to keep families informed about what their children are learning, what they've mastered, and where they might need some extra guidance.

Meeting the Standards

Connections to the Common Core State Standards

The Common Core State Standards Initiative (CCSSI) has outlined learning expectations in English/Language Arts and Mathematics for students at different grade levels. The activities in this book align with the following standards for students in grades K–1. For more information, visit the CCSSI Web site at www.corestandards.org.

Reading Standards: Foundational Skills

Print Concepts

- RF.K.1, RF.1.1. Demonstrate understanding of the organization and basic features of print.
- RF.K.1a. Recognize and name all upper- and lowercase letters of the alphabet.

Phonological Awareness

- RF.K.2, RF.1.2. Demonstrate understanding of spoken words, syllables, and sounds (phonemes).

Phonics and Word Recognition

- RF.K.3, RF.1.3. Know and apply grade-level phonics and word analysis skills in decoding words.

Fluency

- RF.K.4, RF.1.4. Read with sufficient accuracy and fluency to support comprehension.
- RF.1.4a. Read grade-level text with purpose and understanding.
- RF.1.4b. Read grade-level text orally with accuracy, appropriate rate, and expression.
- RF.1.4c. Use context to confirm or self-correct word recognition and understanding, rereading as necessary.

Language

Conventions of Standard English

- L.K.1, L.1.1. Demonstrate command of the conventions of standard English grammar and usage when writing or speaking.
- L.K.1a, L.1.1a. Print upper- and lowercase letters.
- L.K.2, L.1.2. Demonstrate command of the conventions of standard English capitalization, punctuation, and spelling when writing.

Mathematics

Counting & Cardinality

- K.CC.3. Write numbers from 0 to 20.

Geometry

- K.G.2. Correctly name shapes regardless of their orientations or overall size.
- K.G.4. Analyze and compare two-dimensional shapes, in different sizes and orientations.
- 1.G.1 Distinguish between defining attributes (e.g., triangles are closed and three-sided) versus non-defining attributes (e.g., color, orientation, overall size).

Connections to the NCTM Math Standards

The activities also help support you in meeting the following PreK–1 standards—including process standards, such as problem solving, reasoning and proof, and communication—recommended by the National Council of Teachers of Mathematics (NCTM):

Geometry

Analyze characteristics and properties of two-dimensional geometric shapes

- Recognize, name, compare, and sort shapes
- Describe attributes and parts of shapes

Use visualization, spatial reasoning, and geometric modeling to solve problems

- Recognize and represent shapes from different perspectives

Algebra

Understand patterns, relations, and functions

- Recognize, describe, and extend patterns
- Analyze how repeating patterns are generated

Source: National Council of Teachers of Mathematics. (2000). *Principles and Standards for School Mathematics.* Reston, VA: NCTM. www.nctm.org

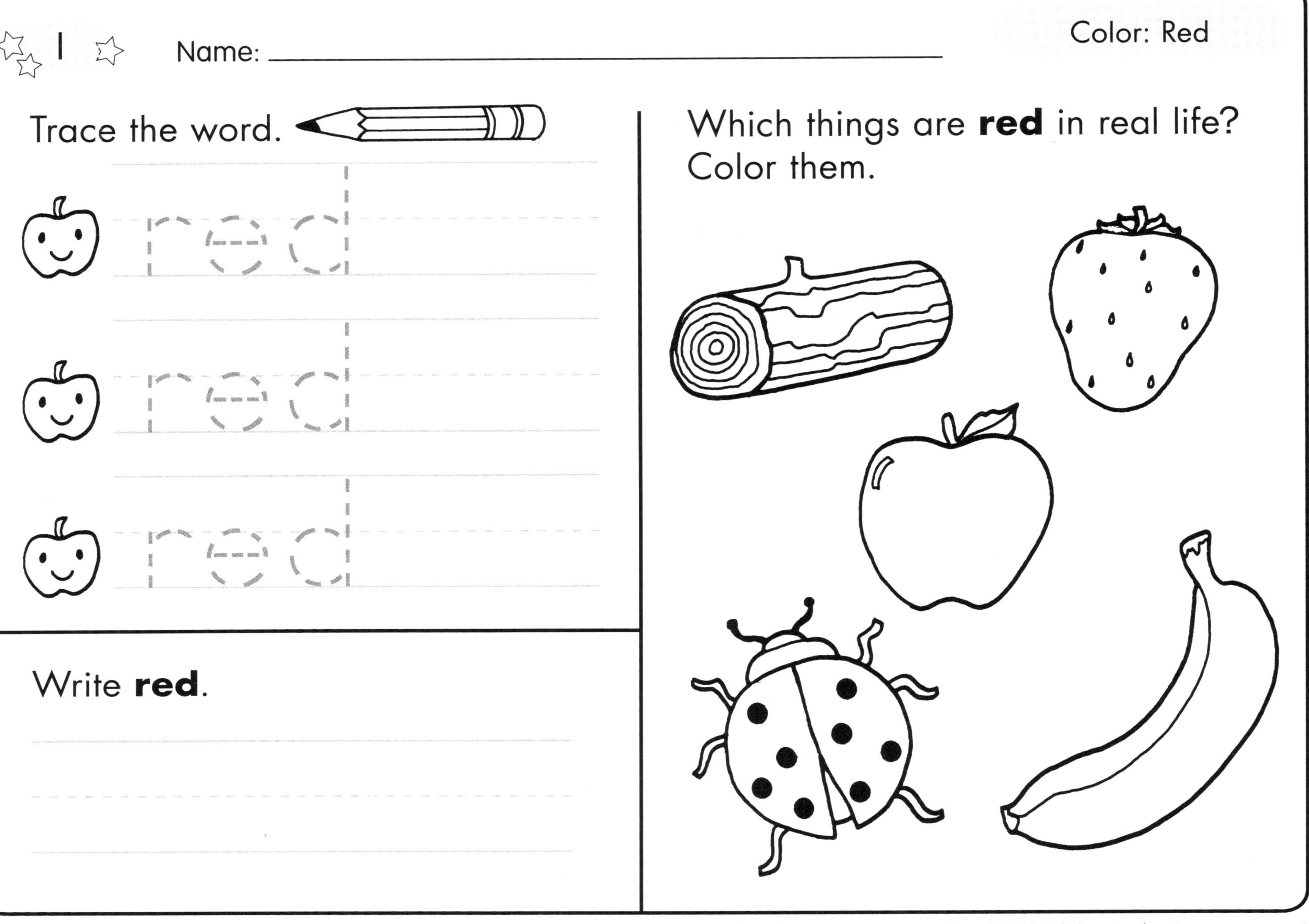

I
Name:
Color: Red
Trace the word.
red
red
red
Write **red**.
Which things are **red** in real life?
Color them.

2 Name: ______________________ Color: Red

Circle each **red**.

| red | run | rot |
| bar | red | red |

Draw a strawberry. Color each strawberry **red**.

Write **red**.

The strawberries are ______________.

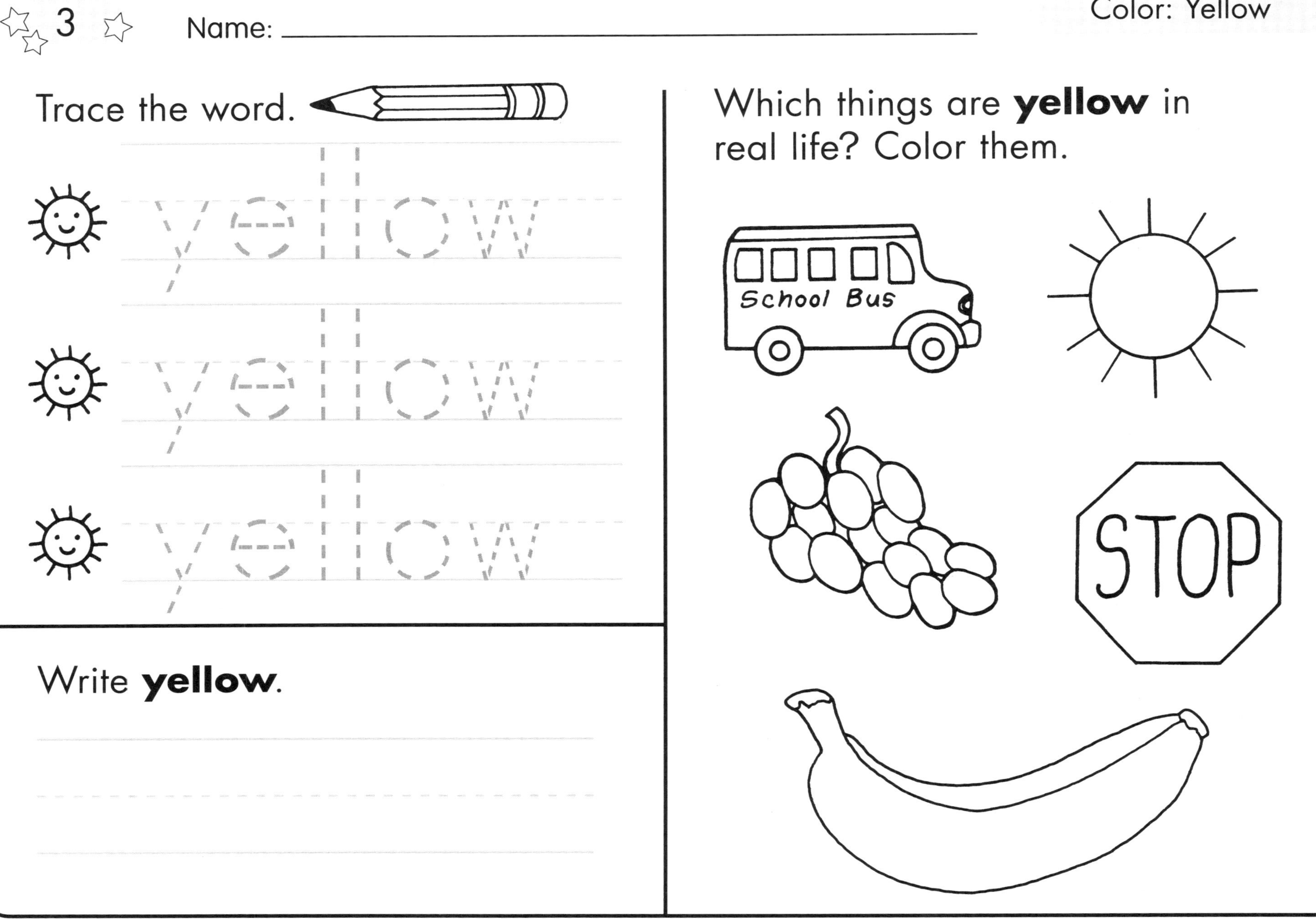
3
Name:
Color: Yellow
Trace the word.
yellow
yellow
yellow
Write **yellow**.
Which things are **yellow** in real life? Color them.
School Bus
STOP

4 Name: ____________________ Color: Yellow

Circle each **yellow**.

wall	yellow	your
yellow	anyhow	yellow

Draw a banana. Color each banana **yellow**.

Write **yellow**.

I want to eat a ____________ banana.

5 Name: ______________________ Color: Blue

Trace the word.

blue

blue

blue

Write **blue**.

Which things are **blue** in real life? Color them.

1st

6 Name: ____________________ Color: Blue

Circle each **blue**.

bulb	ball	blue
blue	blue	bold

Draw a bird. Color each bird **blue**.

Write **blue**.

Watch the ____________ birds fly.

7 Name: ______________________

Color: Green

Trace the word.

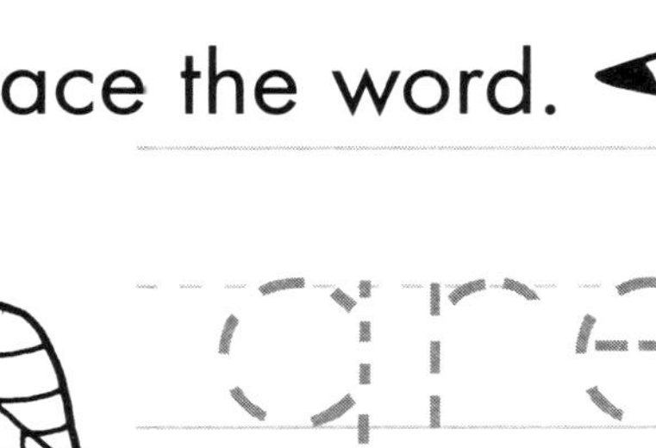

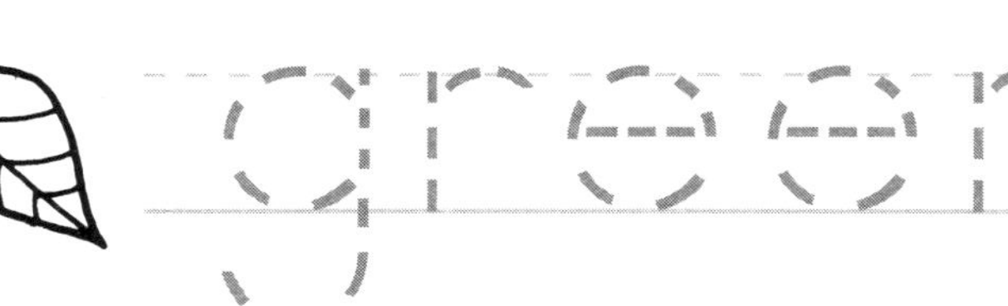

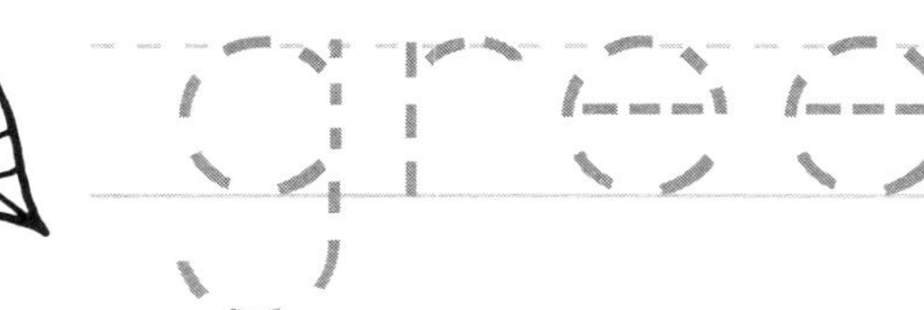

Write **green**.

Which things are **green** in real life? Color them.

8 Name: ____________________ Color: Green

Circle each **green**.

great green green

green seen game

Draw a caterpillar. Color each caterpillar **green**.

Write **green**.

The caterpillars are ____________.

9 Name: ______________________

Color the picture. Use the Color Key.

Color Key

= red	= yellow
= green	= blue

10 Name: ____________________

Write the color for each picture.
Use the words in the box.
Then color the pictures.

blue green yellow red

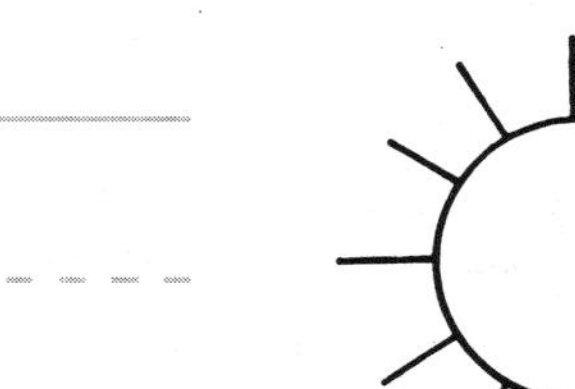

11 Name: ______________________ Color: Orange

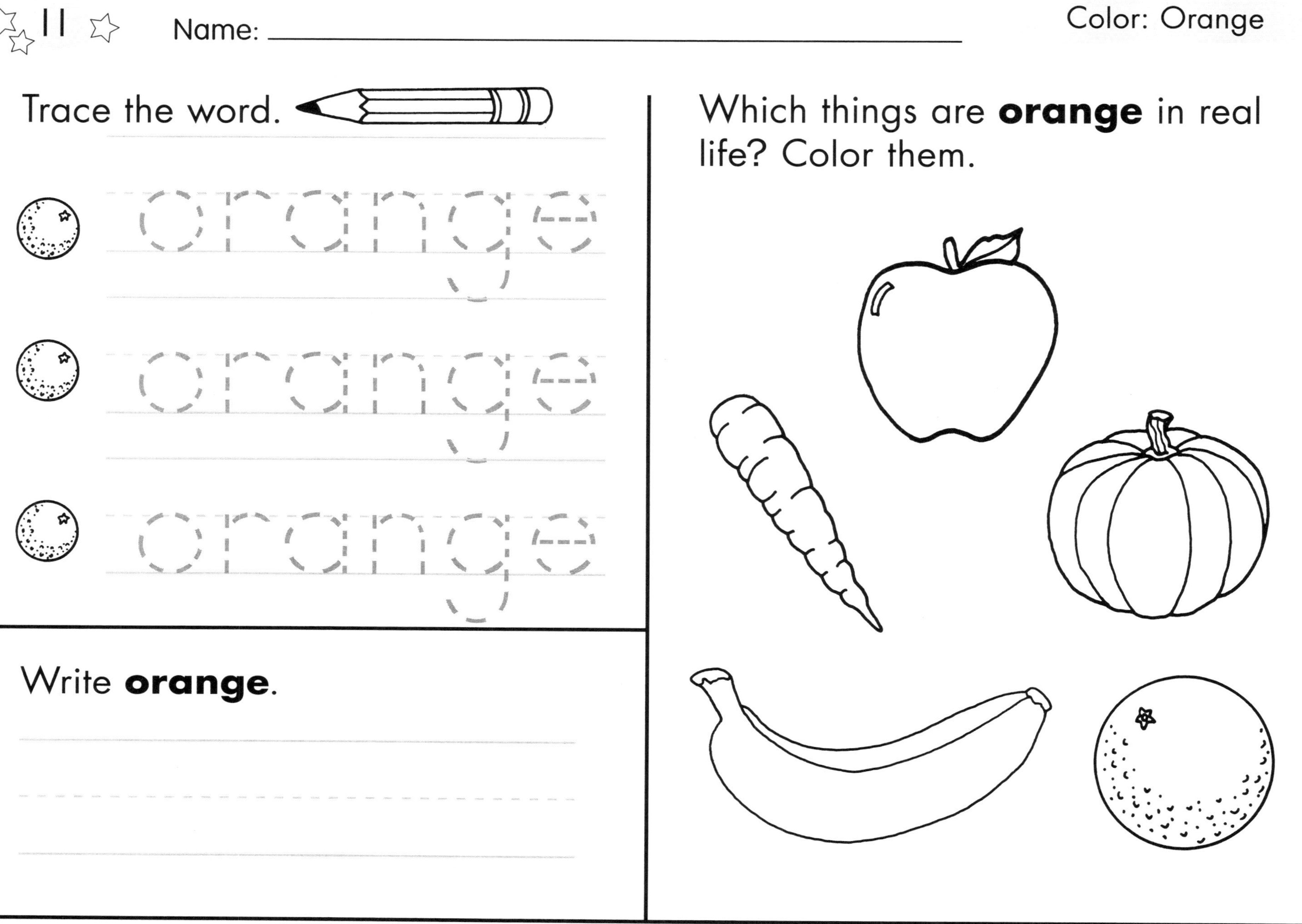

Trace the word.

orange

orange

orange

Which things are **orange** in real life? Color them.

Write **orange**.

12 Name: ______________________ Color: Orange

Circle each **orange**.

orange	grain	orange
grand	orange	cover

Draw a pumpkin. Color each pumpkin **orange**.

Write **orange**.

Look at the big ______________ pumpkins.

13 Name: ____________________ Color: Purple

Trace the word.

purple

purple

purple

Write **purple**.

Which things are **purple** in real life? Color them.

14 Name: ____________________ Color: Purple

Circle each **purple**.

party purple play

quiet purple purple

Draw a bunch of grapes. Color the grapes **purple**.

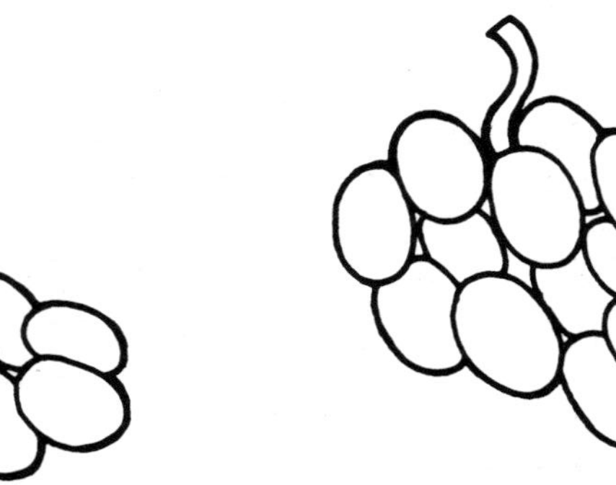

Write **purple**.

Let's eat the ____________________ grapes.

15 Name: ____________________ Color: Black

Trace the word.

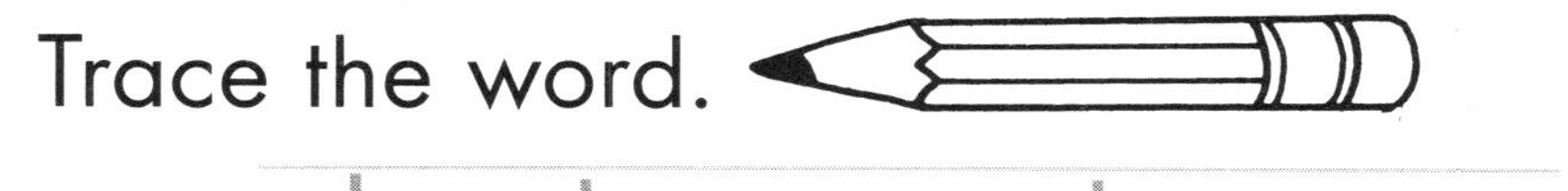

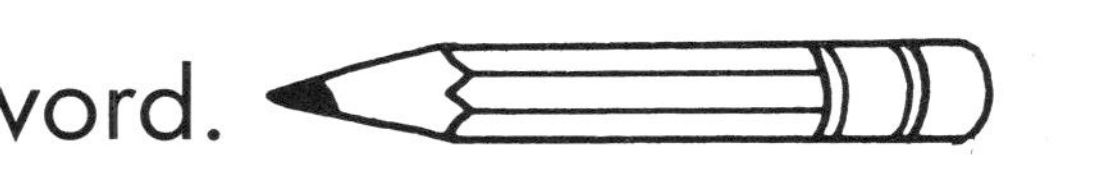

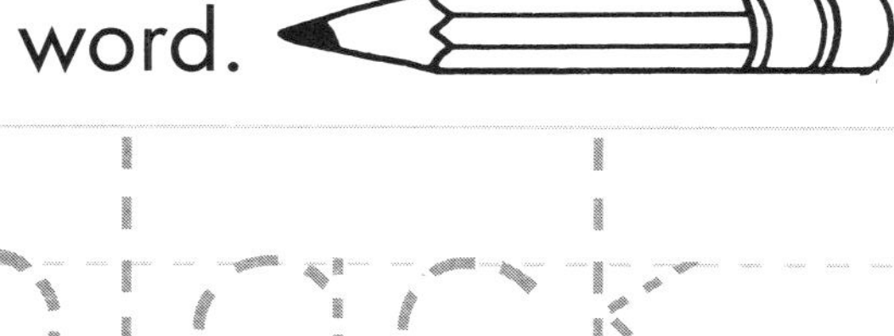

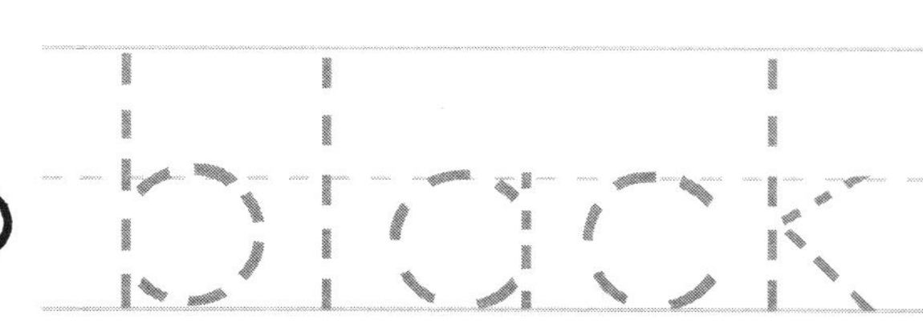

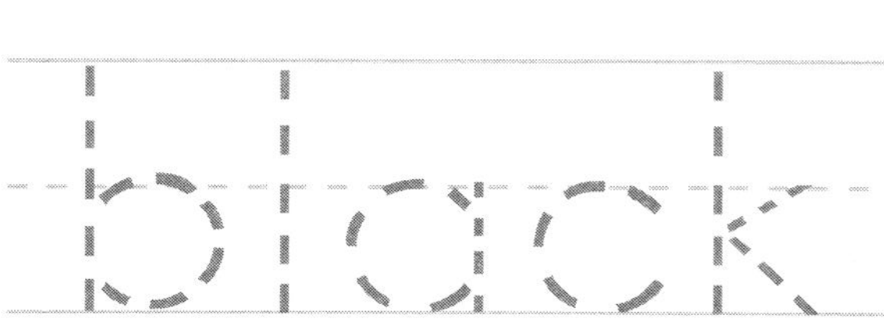

Write **black**.

Which things are **black** in real life? Color them.

16 Name: ______________________ Color: Black

Circle each **black**.

black back black

black bend ball

Draw a crow. Color each crow **black**.

Write **black**.

I see two ______________ crows.

17 Name: ______________________ Color: Brown

Trace the word.

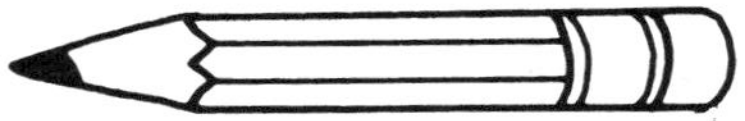

brown

brown

brown

Write **brown**.

Which things are **brown** in real life? Color them.

18 Name: ____________________ Color: Brown

Circle each **brown**.

blow	brown	clown
brown	bring	brown

Draw a bear. Color each bear **brown**.

Write **brown**.

The two big bears are ____________.

19 Name: ____________________

Color the picture. Use the Color Key.

Color Key

= purple = orange

= brown = black

Name: ____________________

Write the color for each picture.
Use the words in the box.
Then color the pictures.

purple	black	brown	orange

____

____

____

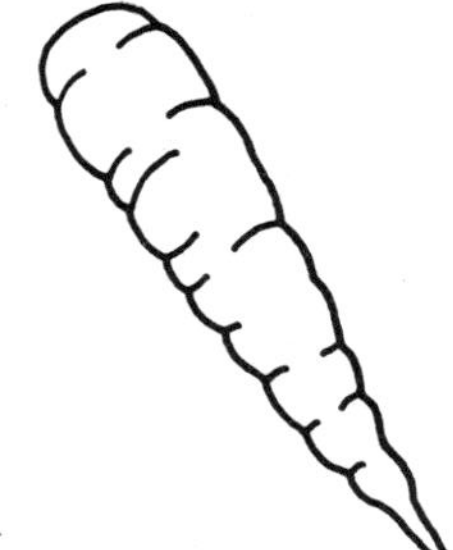

____

Name: ______________________

Color the picture. Use the Color Key.

Color Key

 red

blue

yellow

 green

orange

purple

 black

brown

Color the picture. Use the Color Key.

Color Key

- purple
- red
- orange
- yellow
- green
- brown
- black
- blue

23 Name: ______________________

Make a color pattern
in each row.
Use the Color Key.

Color Key

 = red  = blue  = yellow

1.      

2.      

3.     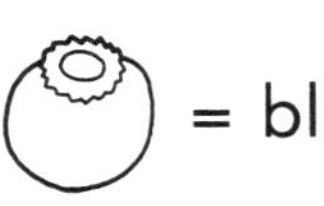 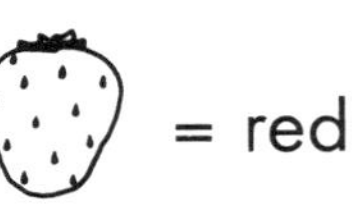

Name: ______________________________

Make a color pattern
in each row.
Use the Color Key.

Color Key

= red  = yellow  = green

1.        

2.        

3.  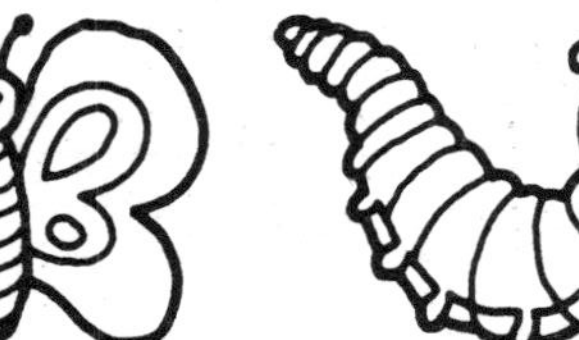  

25 Name: ____________________

Make a color pattern
in each row.
Use the Color Key.

Color Key

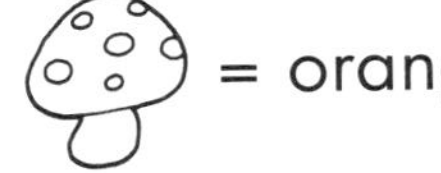 = purple 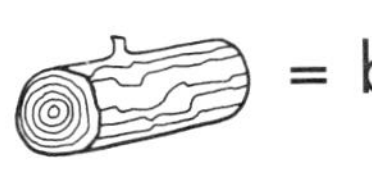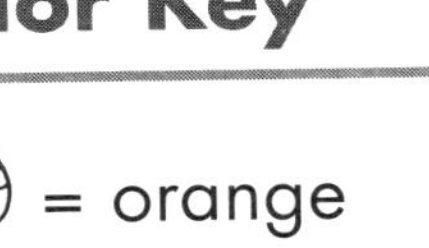 = orange  = brown

1. 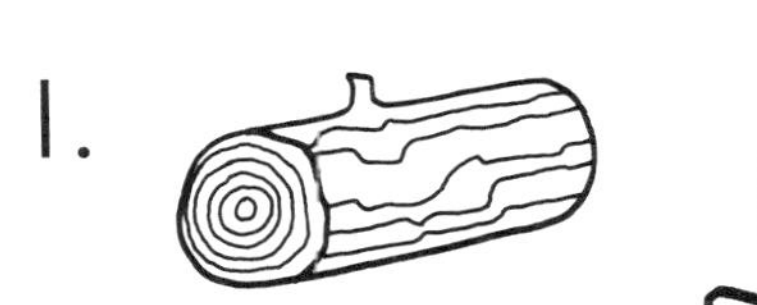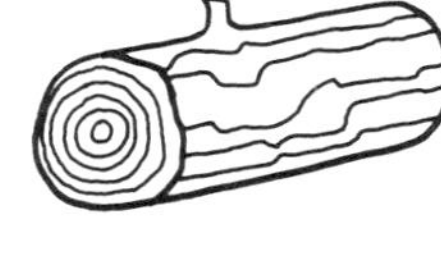

2. 

3. 

Name: ______________________

Make a color pattern
in each row.
Use the Color Key.

Color Key

= purple  = black  = brown

1.

2.

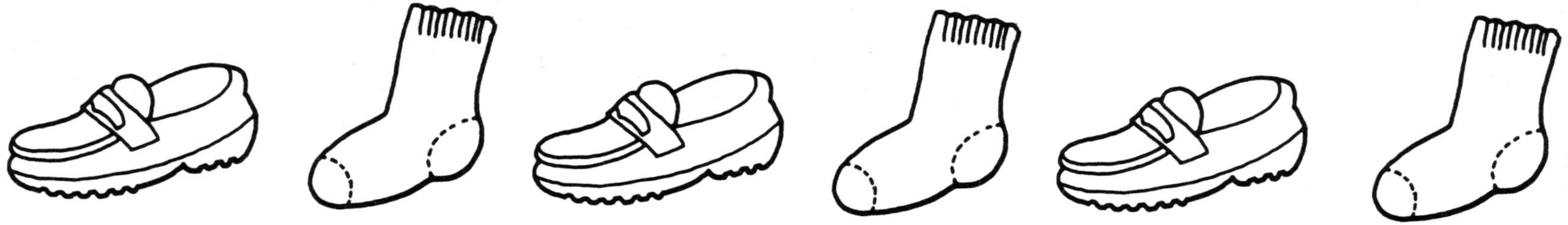

3.

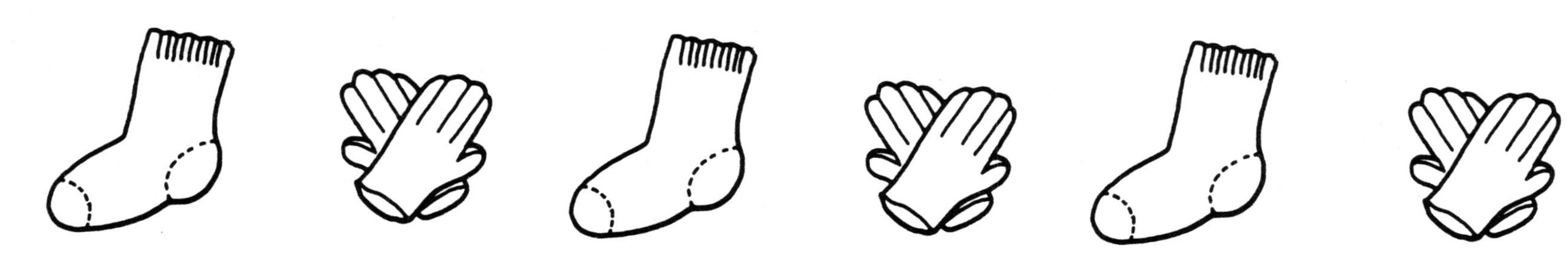

Name: ____________________

Make a color pattern in each row.
Use the Color Key.

Color Key

(balloon) = red (party hat) = orange (gift box) = blue

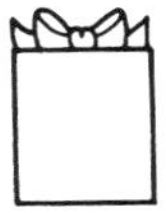

1.

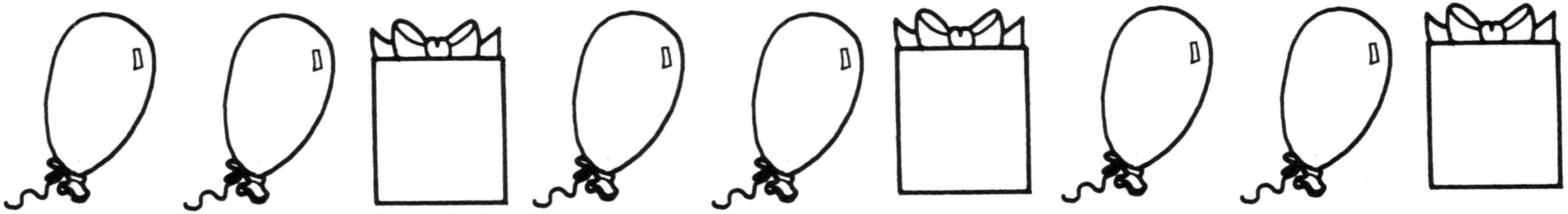

2.

3.

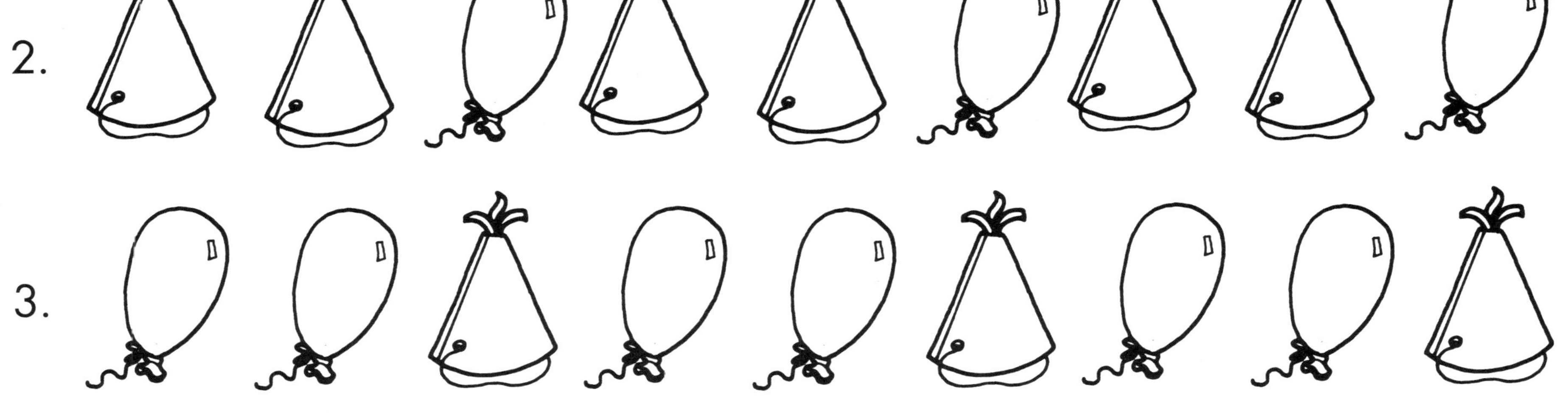

Name: ______________________________

Make a color pattern
in each row.
Use the Color Key.

Color Key

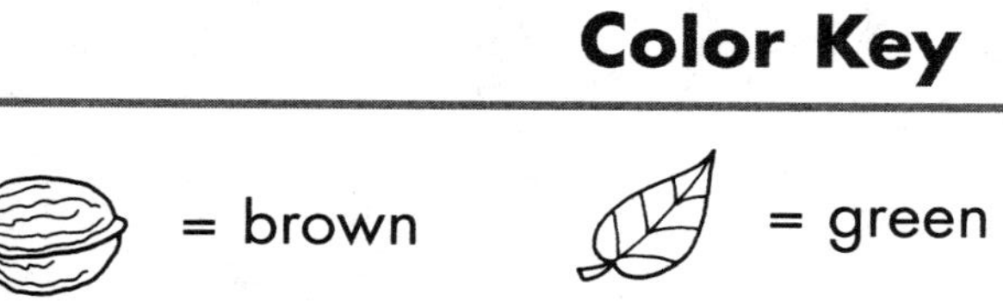
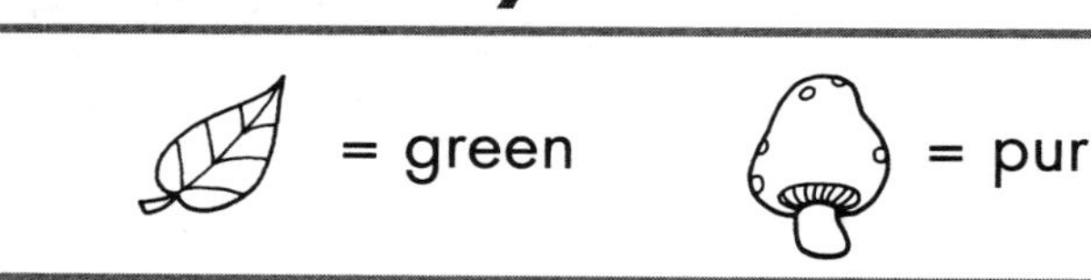

= brown = green = purple

1. 

2. 

3. 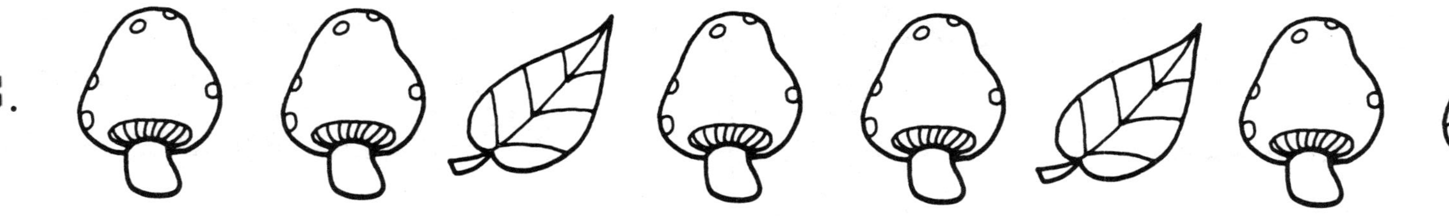
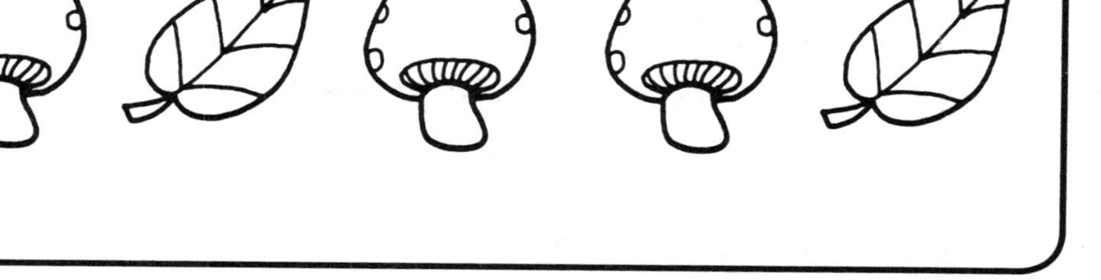

Name: ____________________

Make a color pattern
in each row.
Use the Color Key.

Color Key

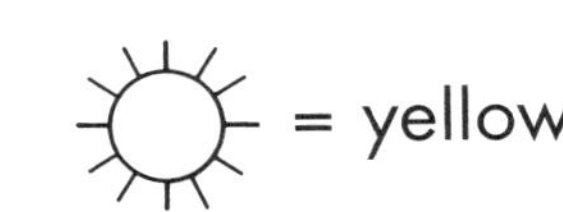 = yellow   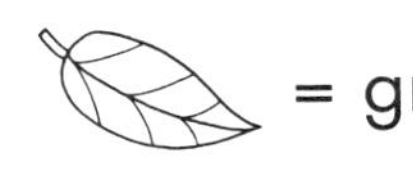 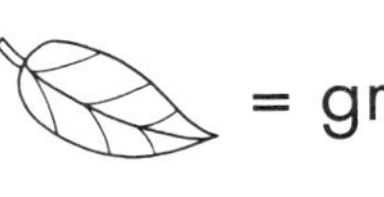 = blue   = green

1. 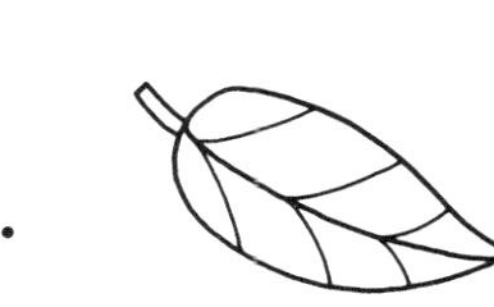 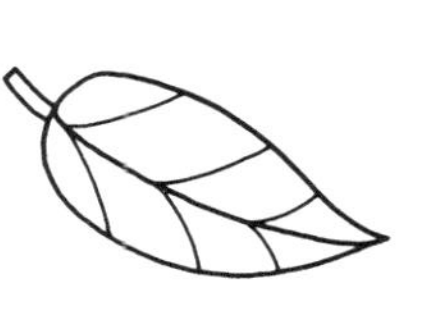 

2.    

3. 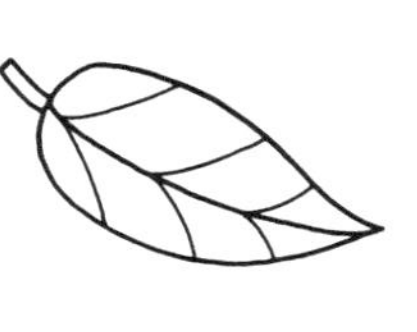 

4.     

Name: ____________________

Make a color pattern
in each row.
Use the Color Key.

Color Key

= black    = red    = purple

1.

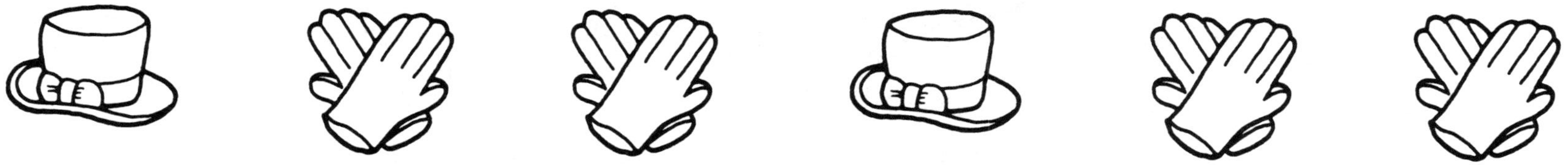

2.

3.

4.

Make a color pattern
in each row.
Use the Color Key.

Color Key

= green = red = yellow

1.

2.

3.

4.

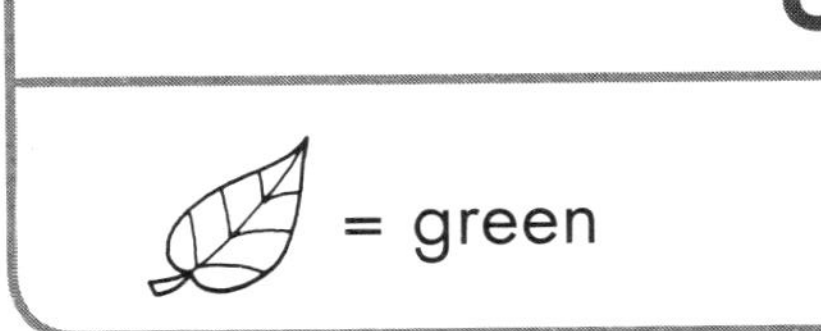
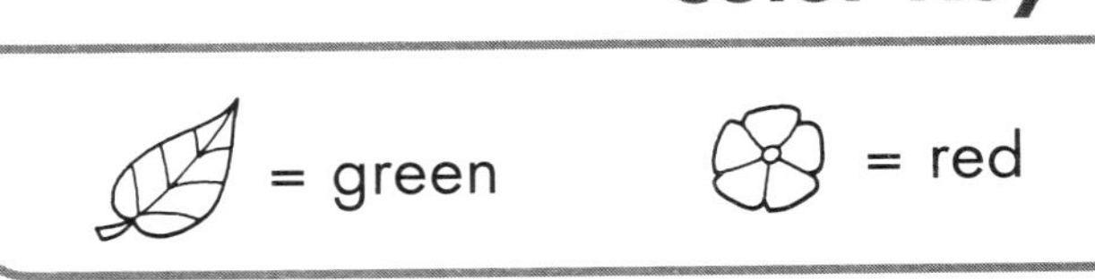

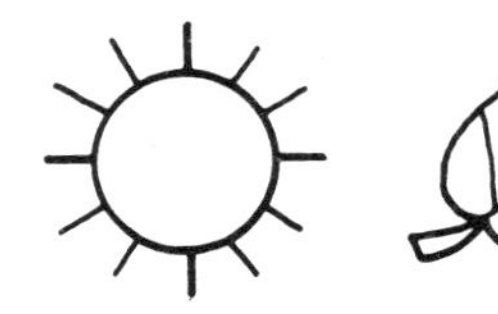
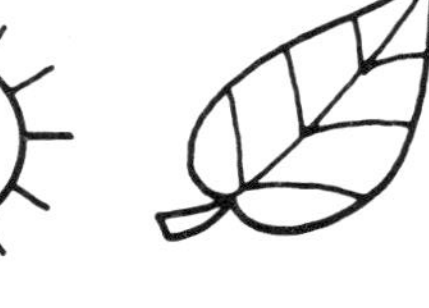

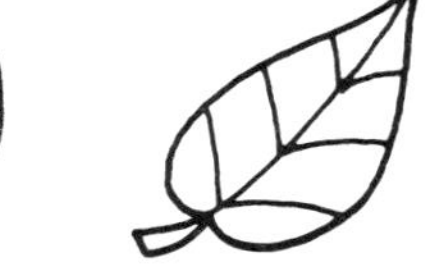

Name: ____________________

Make a color pattern
in each row.
Use the Color Key.

Color Key

 = blue 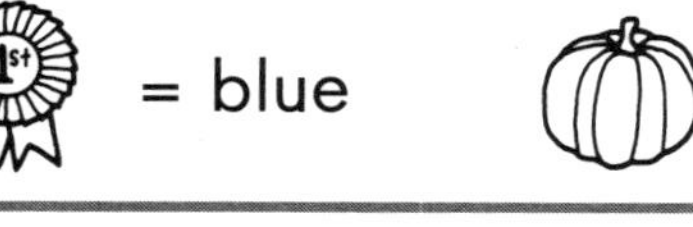 = orange  = brown

1.      

2.      

3.     

4.    

Name: ______________________________

Make a color pattern
in each row.
Use the Color Key.

Color Key

 = purple  = brown 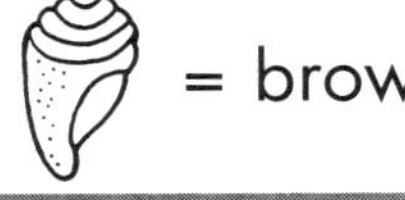 = yellow

1.      

2.      

3.      

4.   

Name: ______________________

Make a color pattern
in each row.
Use the Color Key.

Color Key

= red = orange = yellow

1\.

2\.

3\.

4\.

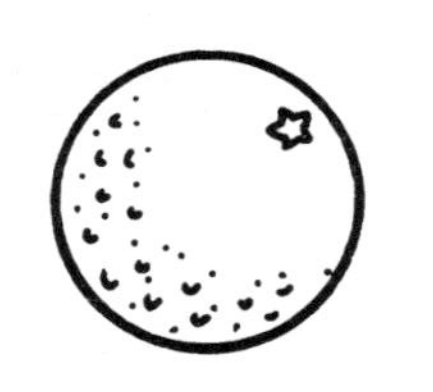
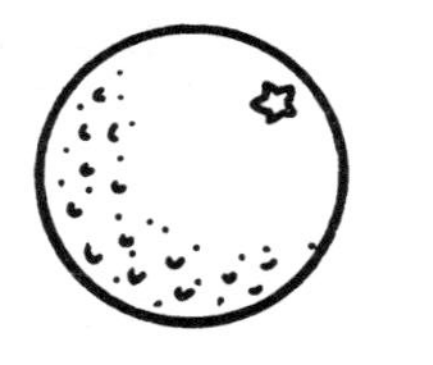

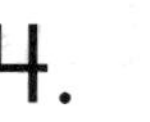

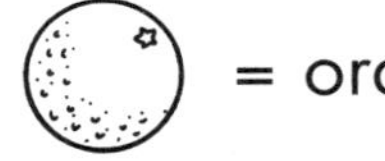

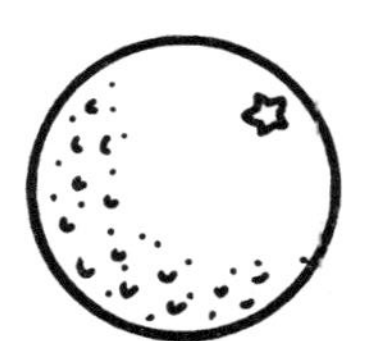

35 Name: ______________________________ Shape: Circle

Trace each **circle**.

Color each **circle**.

36 Name: ______________________ Shape: Circle

Trace the word.

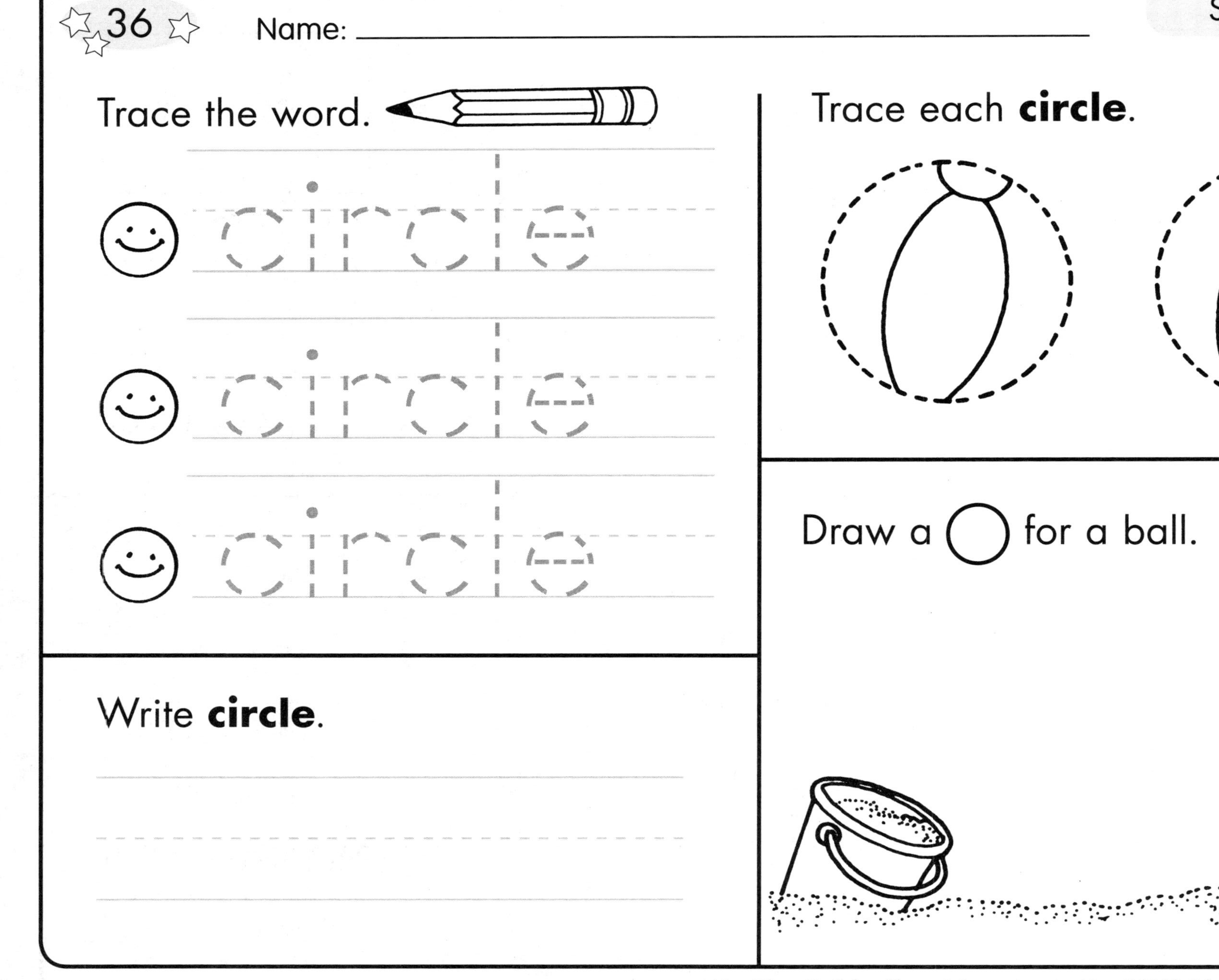

Trace each **circle**.

Draw a ◯ for a ball.

Write **circle**.

37

Name: ______________________________

Shape: Square

Trace each **square**.

Color each **square**.

38 Name: ____________________

Trace the word.

square

square

square

Write **square**.

Trace each **square**.

Draw a □ for a window.

39 Name: ____________________ Shape: Triangle

Trace each **triangle**.

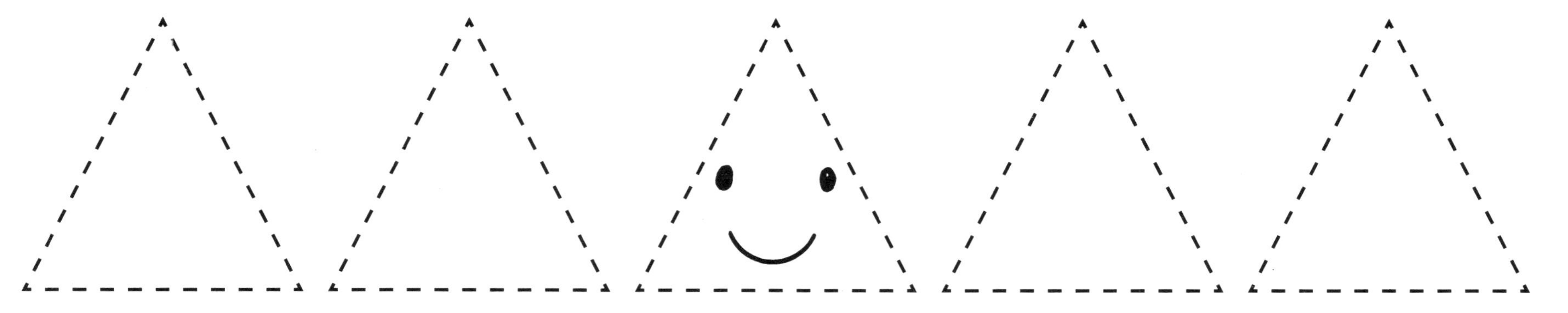

Color each **triangle**.

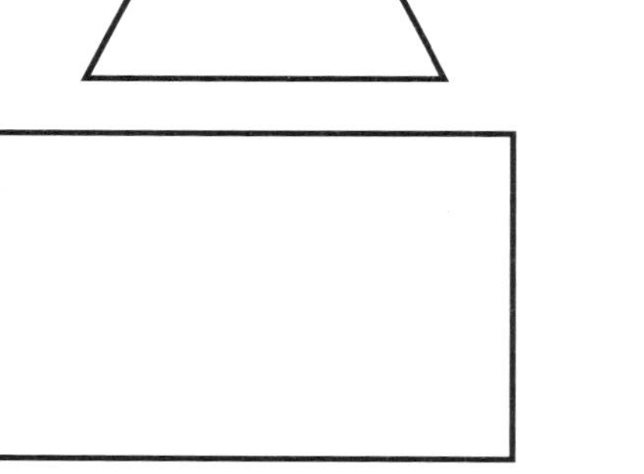

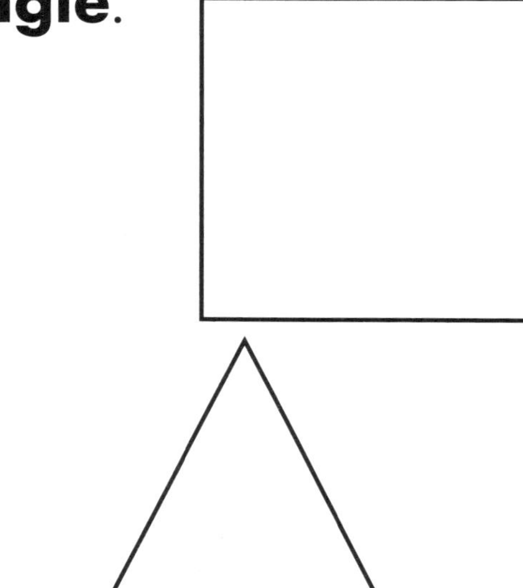

40

Name: ______________________

Shape: Triangle

Trace the word.

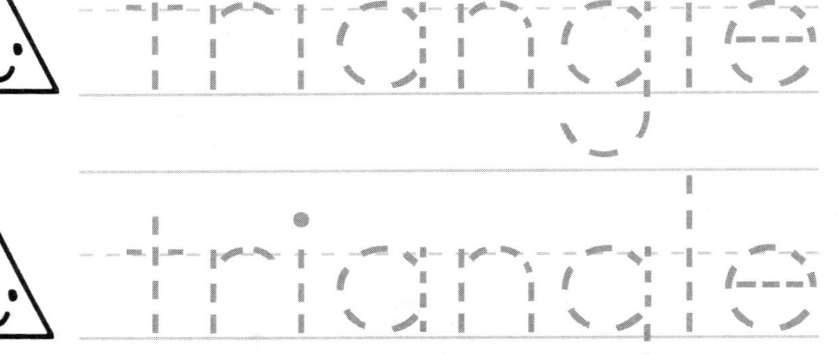

triangle

triangle

triangle

Write **triangle**.

Trace each **triangle**.

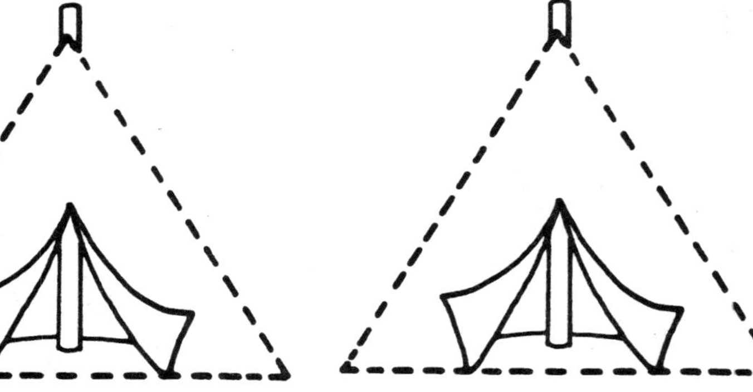

Draw a △ for a tent.

41 Name: ______________________ Shape: Rectangle

Trace each **rectangle**.

Color each **rectangle**.

42 Name: ____________________

Shape: Rectangle

Trace the word.

rectangle

rectangle

rectangle

Write **rectangle**.

Trace each **rectangle**.

Draw a ▭ for a gift.

43 Name: ______________________

Color the picture. Use the Color Key.

Color Key

- ○ green
- □ red
- △ blue
- ▭ brown

Name: ______________________

Write the name for each shape.
Use the words in the box.

square circle rectangle triangle

45 Name: ____________________ Shape: Oval

Trace each **oval**.

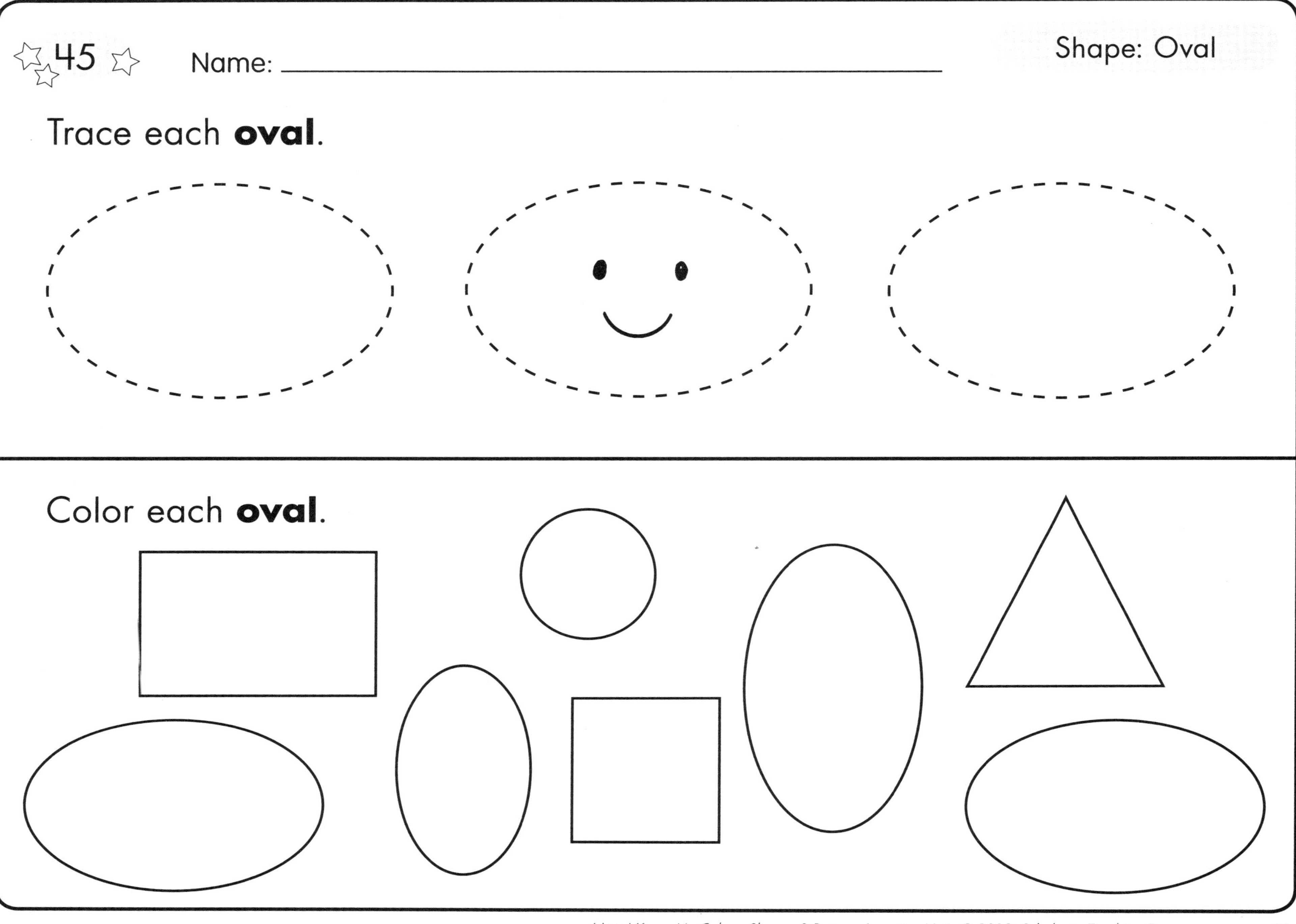

Color each **oval**.

46

Name: ______________________

Shape: Oval

Trace the word.

oval

oval

oval

Write **oval**.

Trace each **oval**.

Draw an ◯ for a pond.

47 Name: ______________________ Shape: Octagon

Trace each **octagon**.

Color each **octagon**.

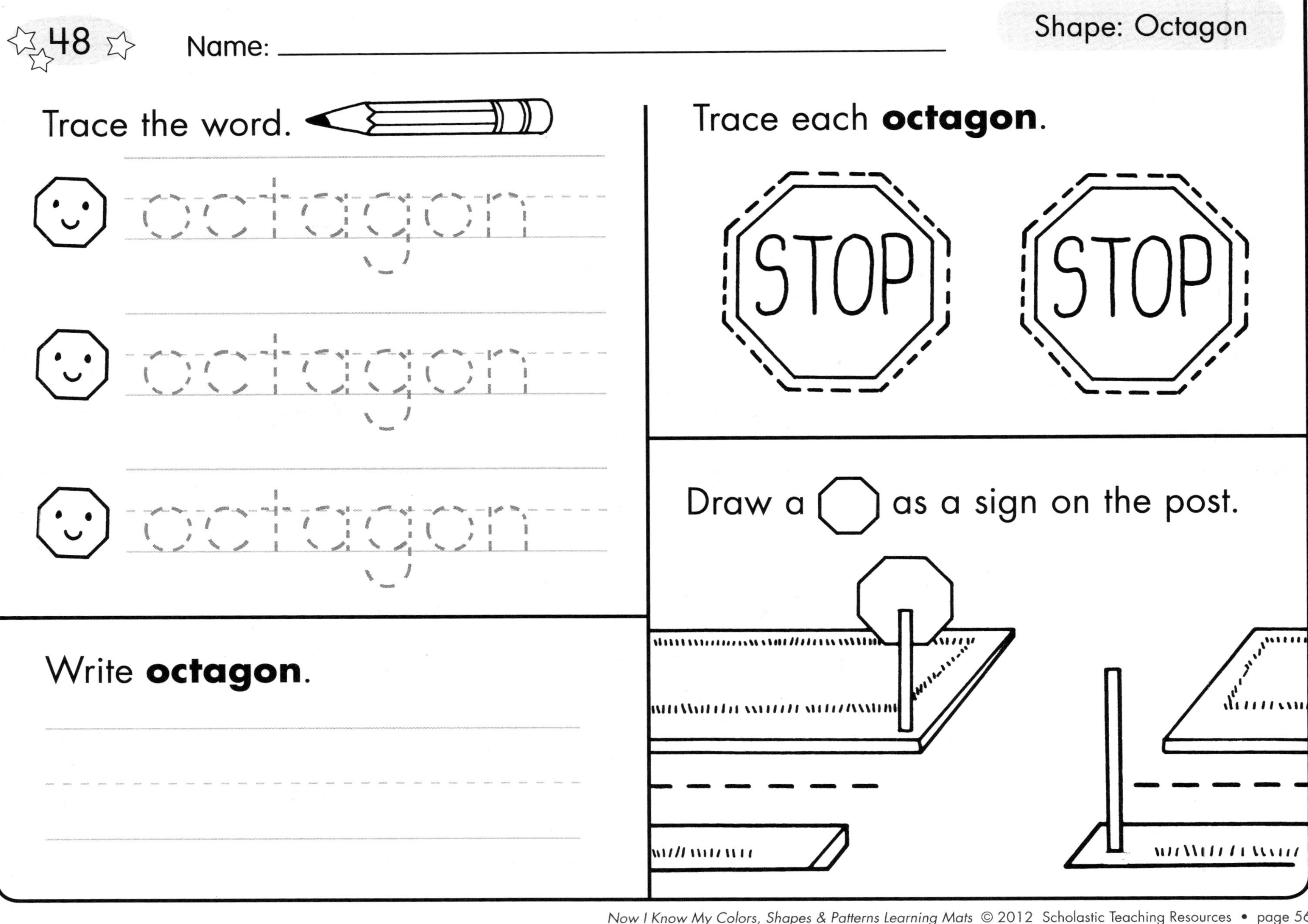
48
Name:
Shape: Octagon
Trace the word.
octagon
octagon
octagon
Trace each **octagon**.
STOP
STOP
Draw a as a sign on the post.
Write **octagon**.

49 Name: ______________________ Shape: Star

Trace each **star**.

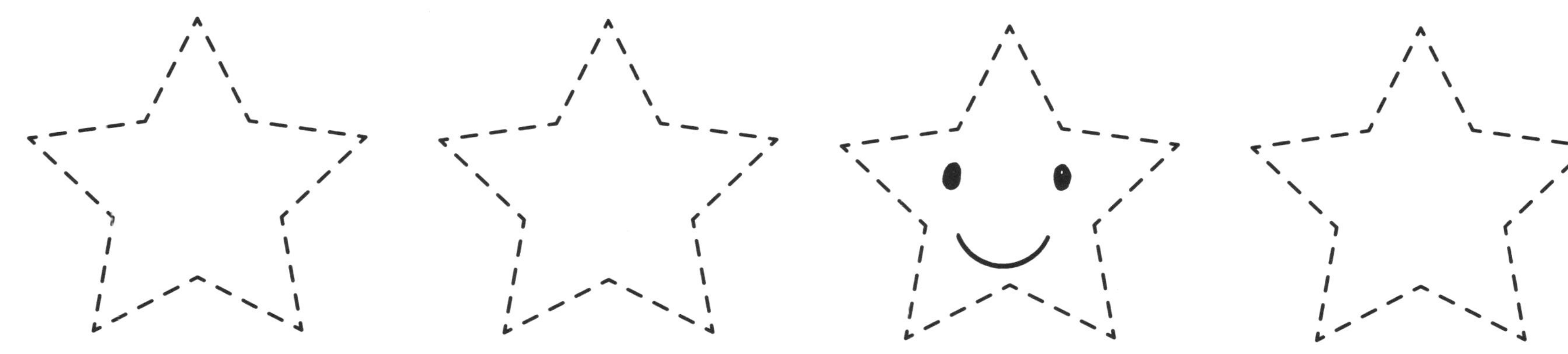

Color each **star**.

50

Name: ______

Shape: Star

Trace the word.

star

star

star

Write **star**.

Trace each **star**.

Draw a ☆ in the sky.

51 Name: ____________________ Shape: Diamond

Trace each **diamond**.

Color each **diamond**.

52 Name: ____________________ Shape: Diamond

Trace the word.

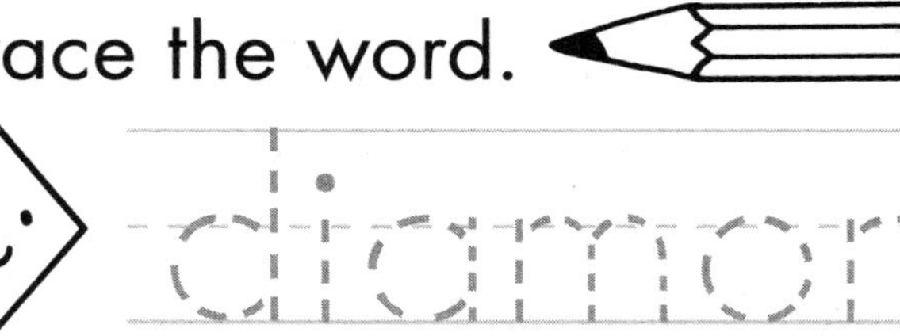

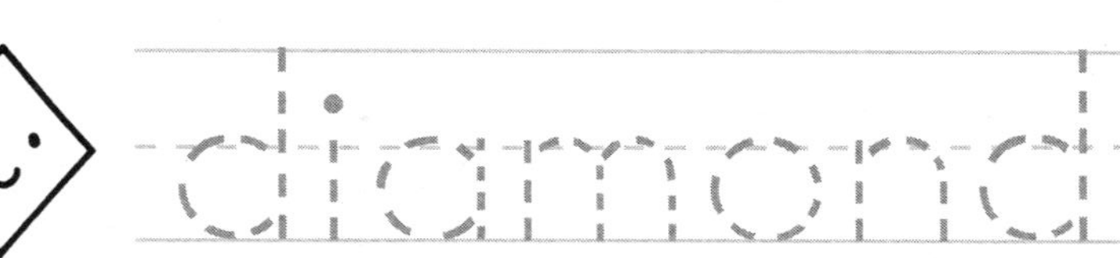

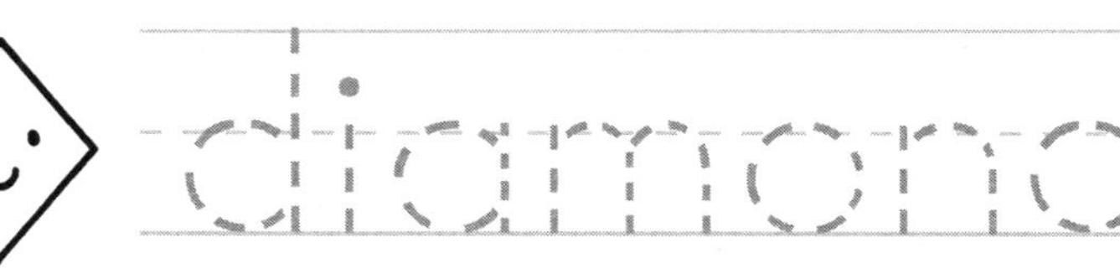

Write **diamond**.

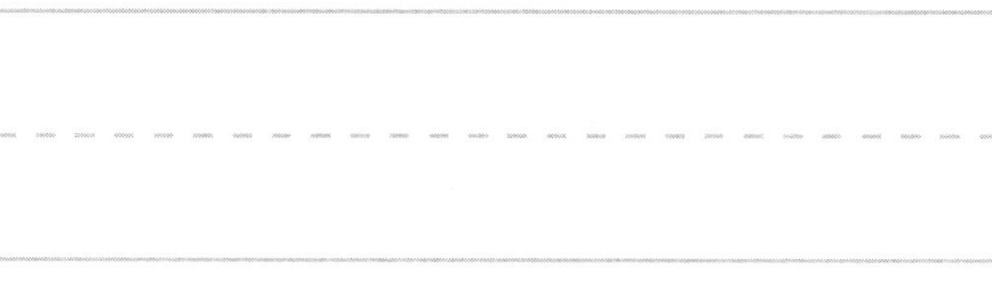

Trace each **diamond**.

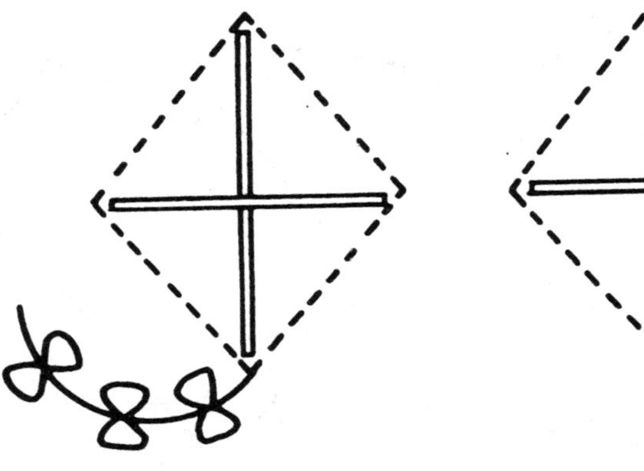

Draw a ◇ for a kite.

Color the picture. Use the Color Key.

Color Key

- blue
- red
- yellow
- green

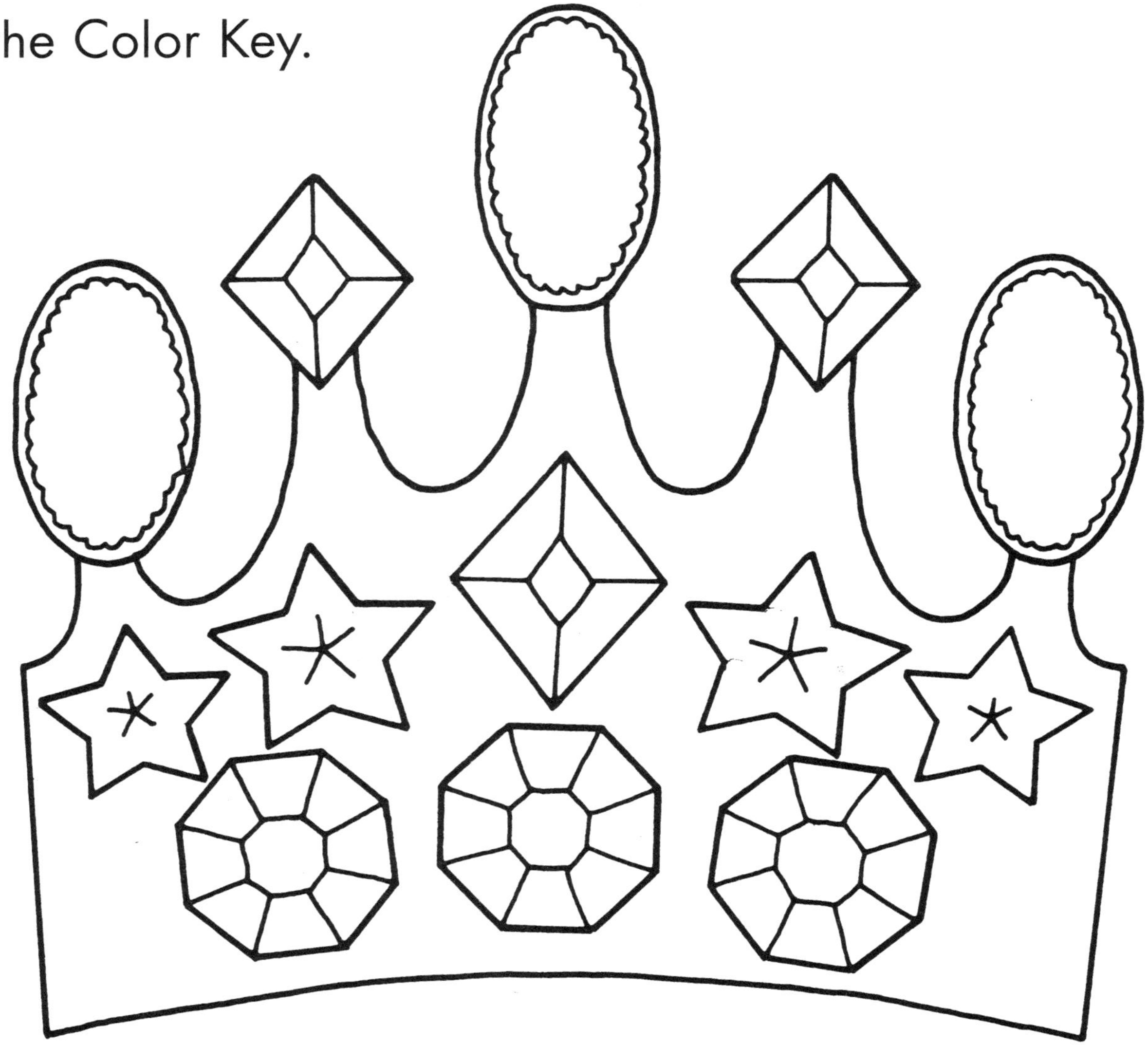

Name: ______________________________

Write the name for each shape.
Use the words in the box.

octagon	oval	diamond	star

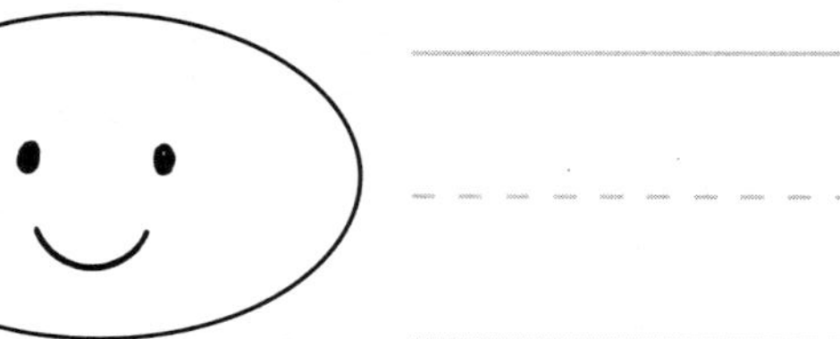

55

Name: ____________________

Draw shapes to complete each pattern.

1.    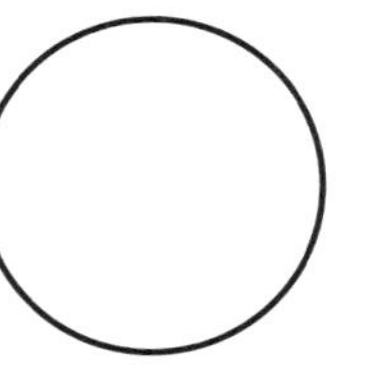        ______ ______

2. 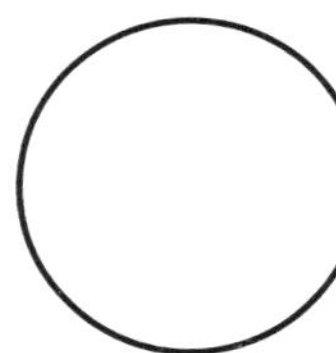 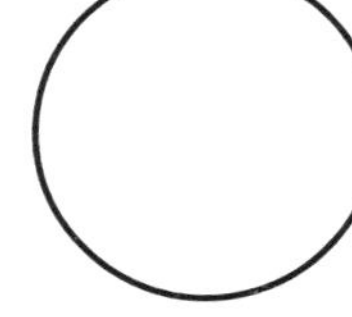 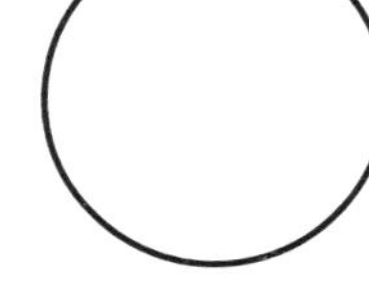 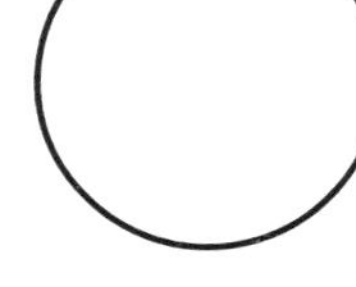 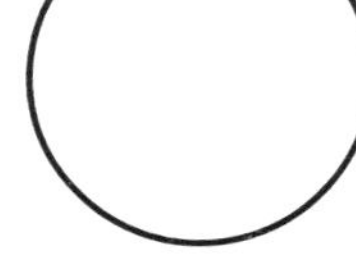 ______ ______

3.        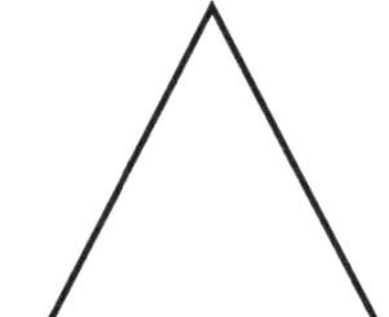 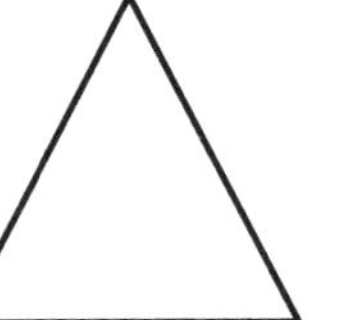 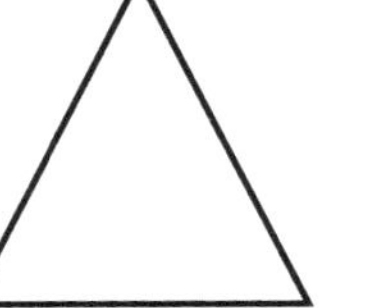 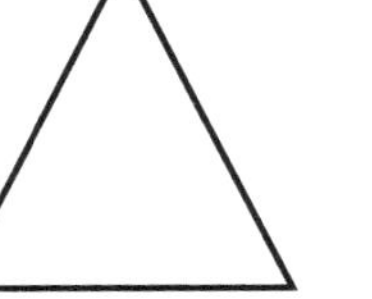 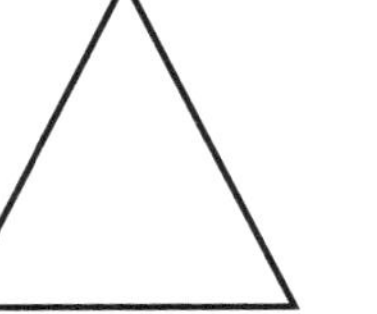 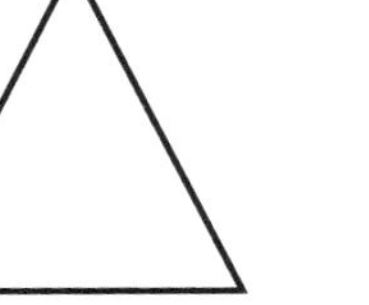 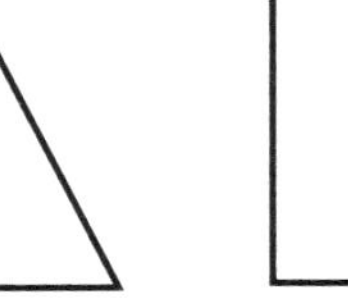 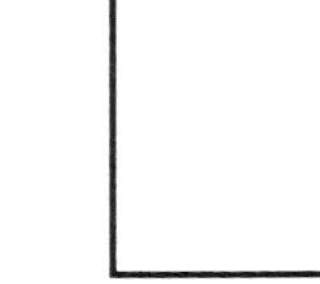   ______ ______

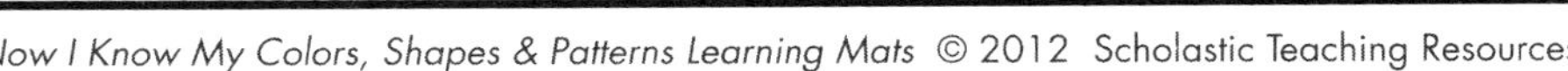

Name: ____________________

Draw shapes to complete each pattern.

1.  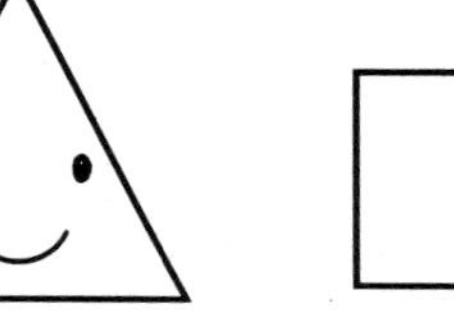 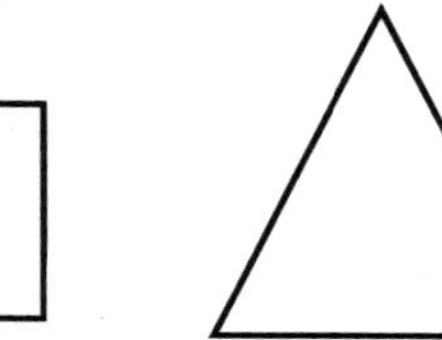 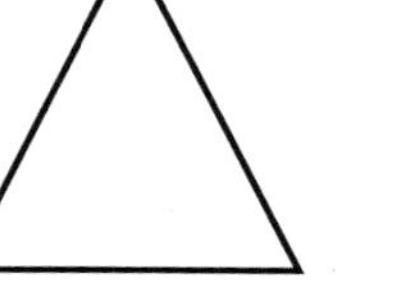 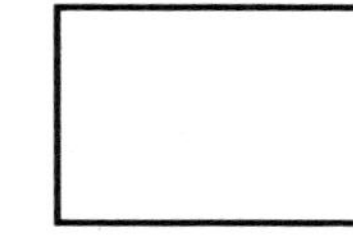 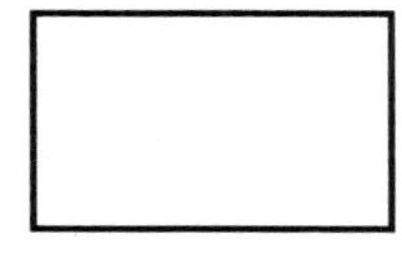  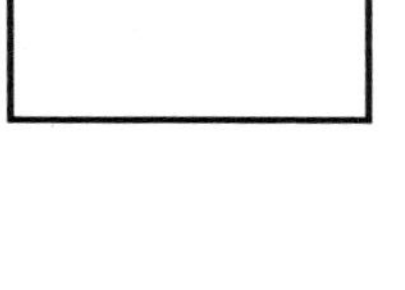 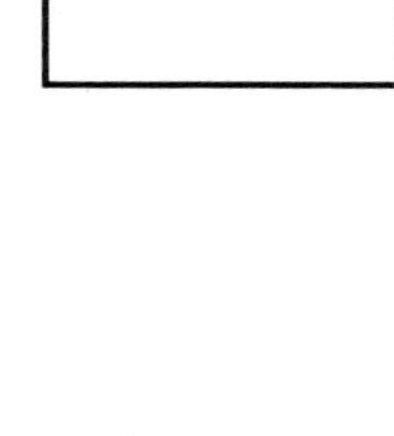 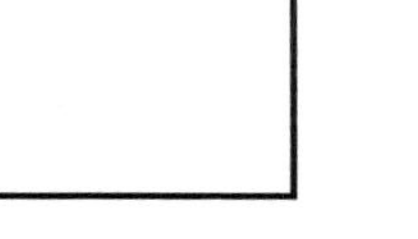 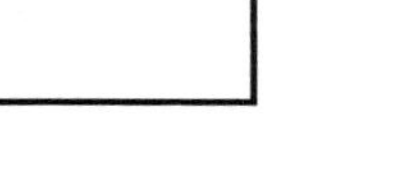 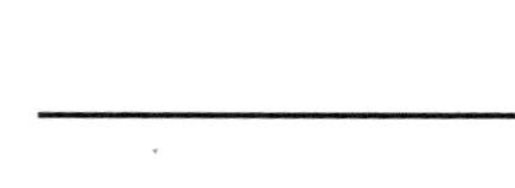 ________ ________

2.      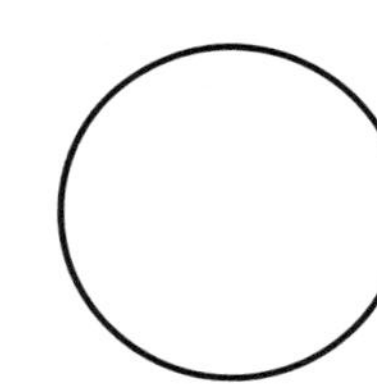 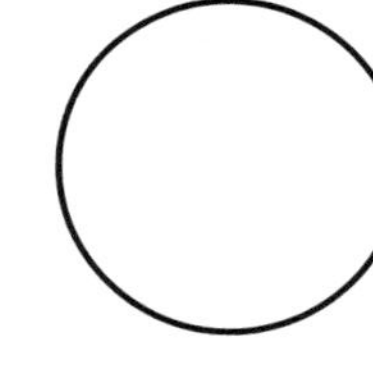 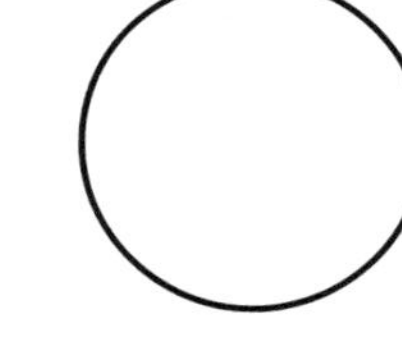 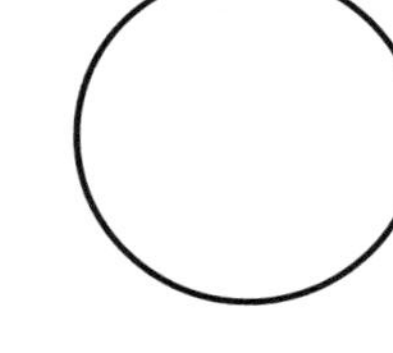 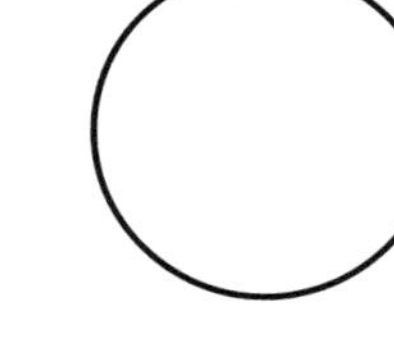 ________ ________

3. 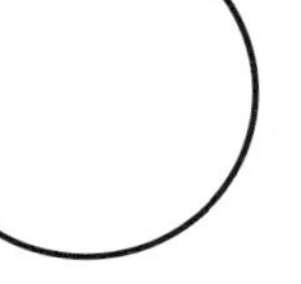 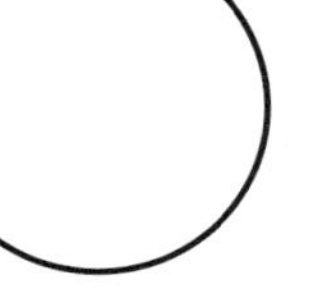 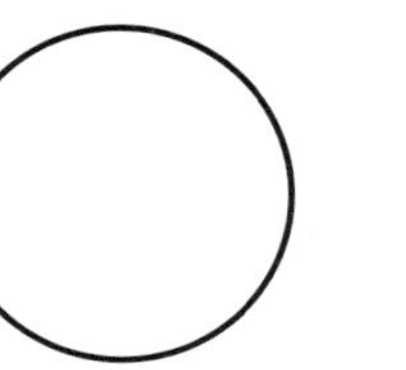 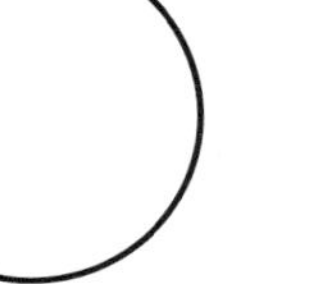   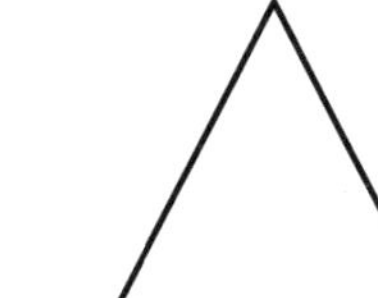   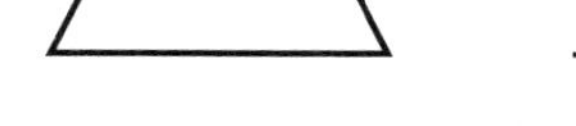 ________ ________

57 Name: ______________________ Shape Patterns: AB

Draw shapes to complete each pattern.

1. ______ ______

2. ______ ______

3. ______ ______

Name: ____________________

Draw shapes to complete each pattern.

1.   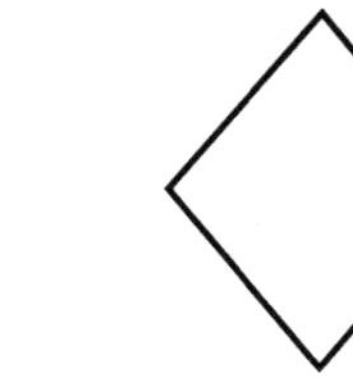   ________ ________

2. 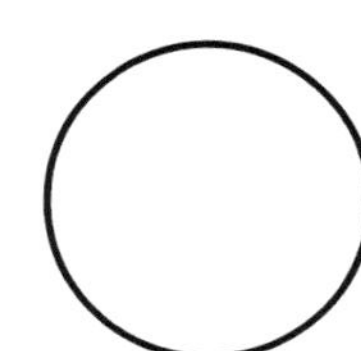 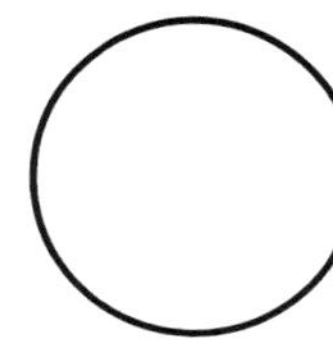 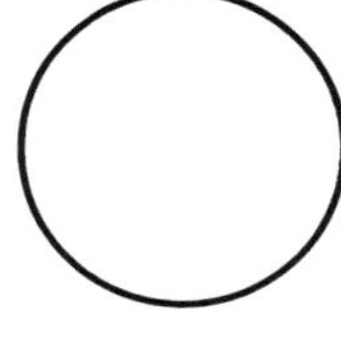  ________ ________

3. 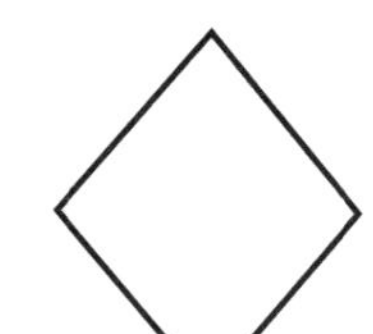 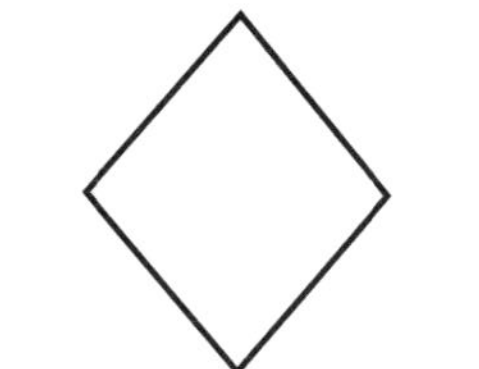 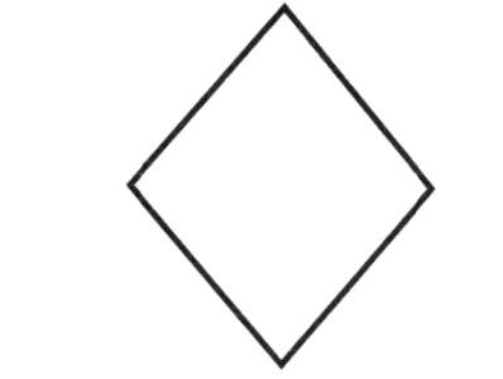 ________ ________

59 Name: ______________________

Draw shapes to complete each pattern.

1. ______ ______ ______

2. ______ ______ ______

3. ______ ______ ______

Draw shapes to complete each pattern.

1.   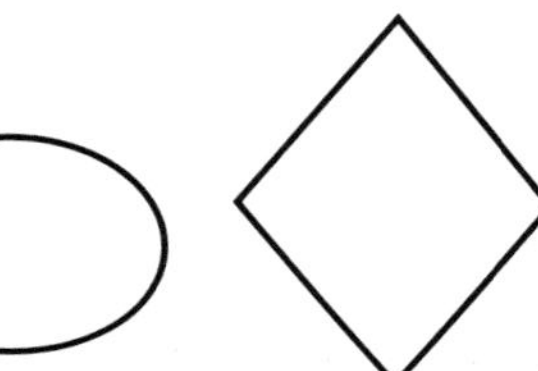 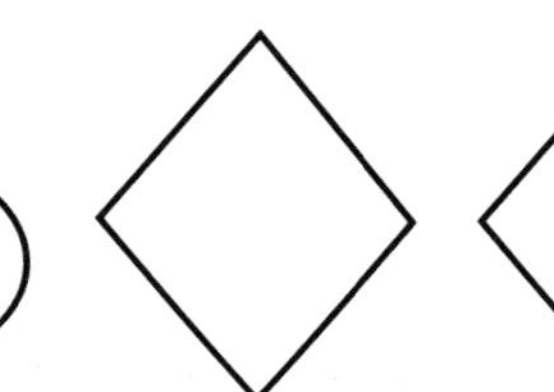 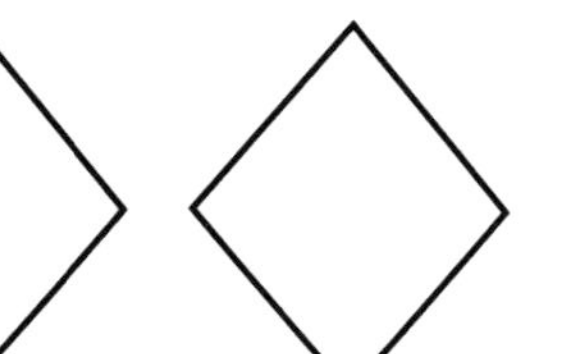 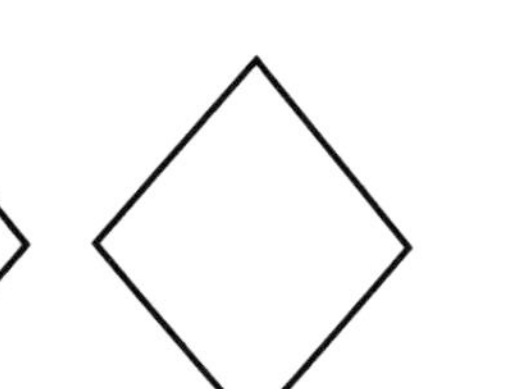  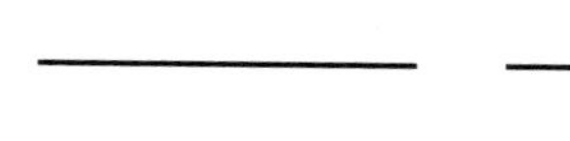 ______ ______ ______

2. 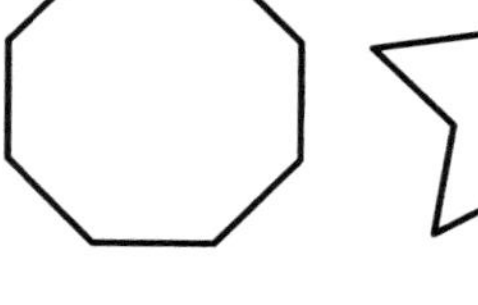 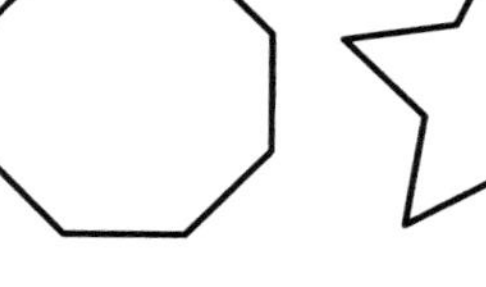 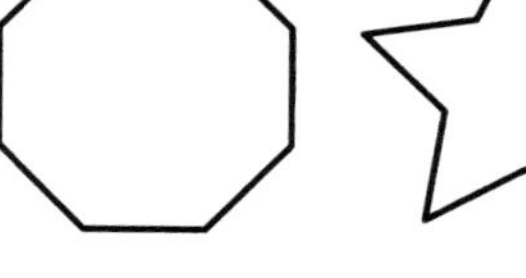     ______ ______ ______

3. 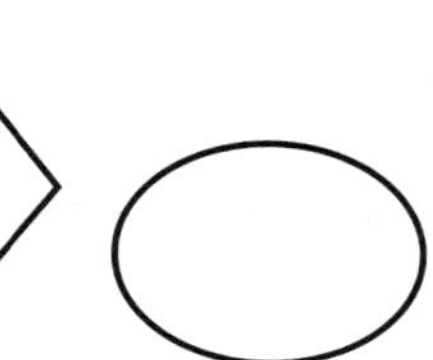 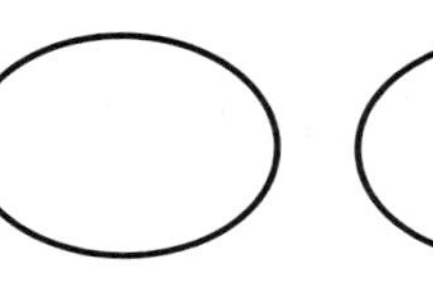 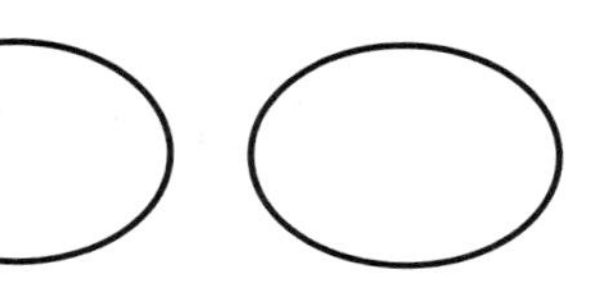 ______ ______ ______

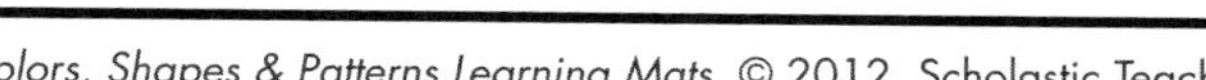

61 Name: ____________________

Shape Patterns: ABB

Draw shapes to complete each pattern.

1. ______ ______ ______

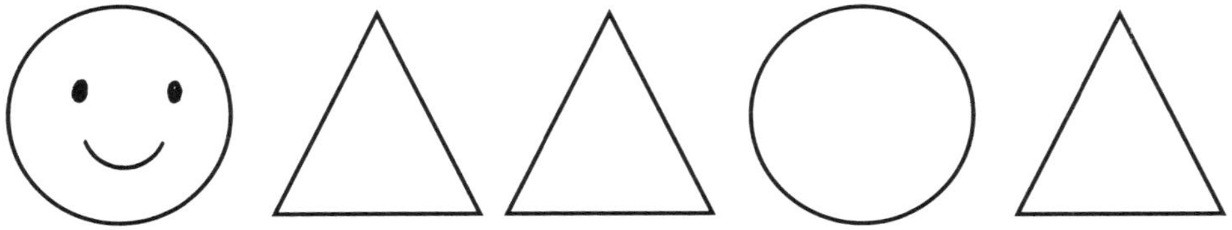

2. ______ ______ ______

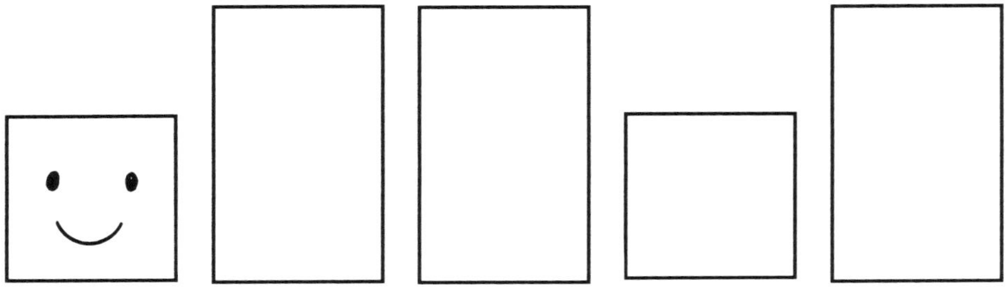

3. ______ ______ ______

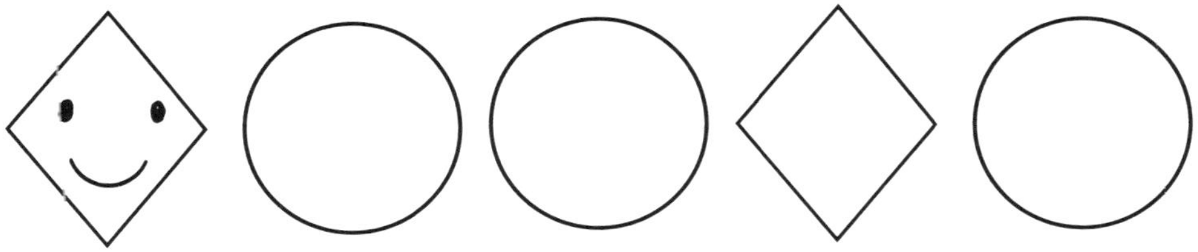

Name: ______________________

Shape Patterns: ABB

Draw shapes to complete each pattern.

1.  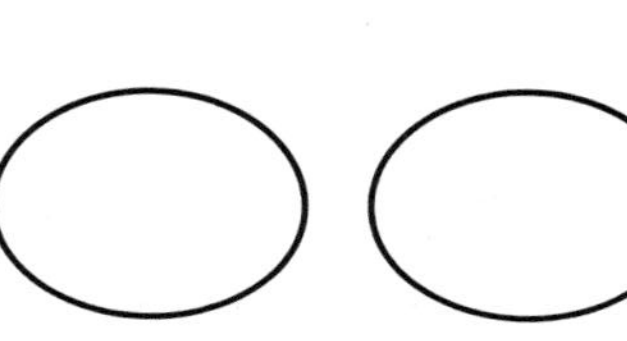 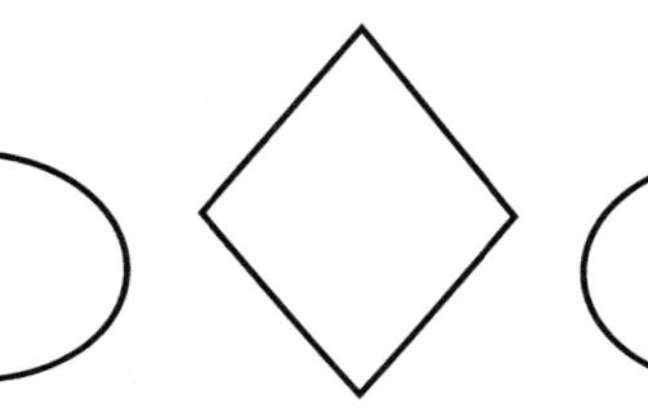 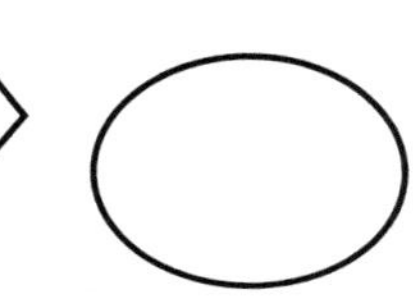 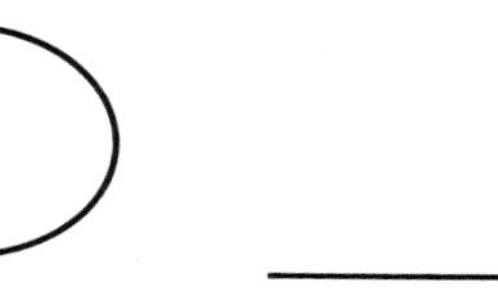  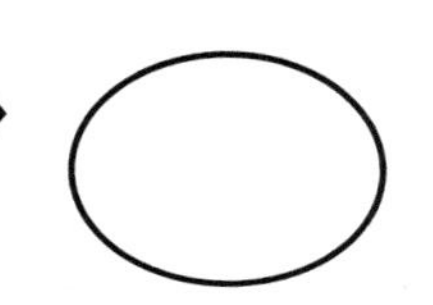 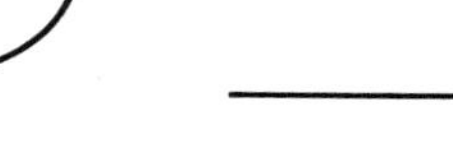 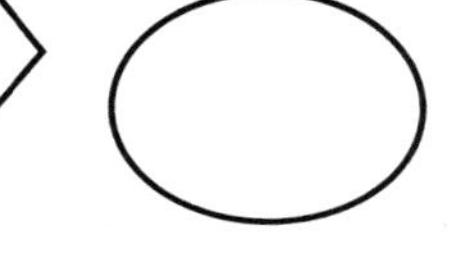   ______ ______ ______

2. 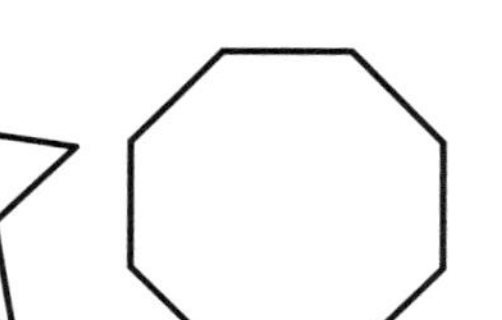 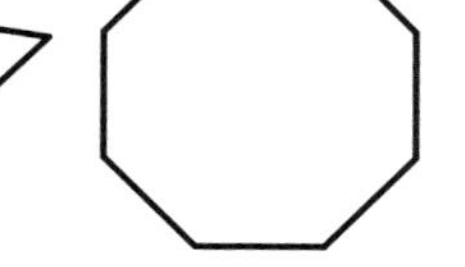   ______ ______ ______

3. 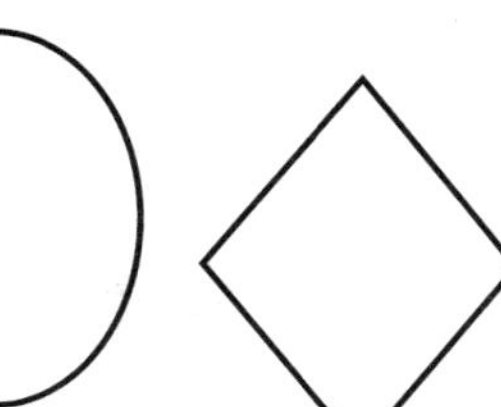   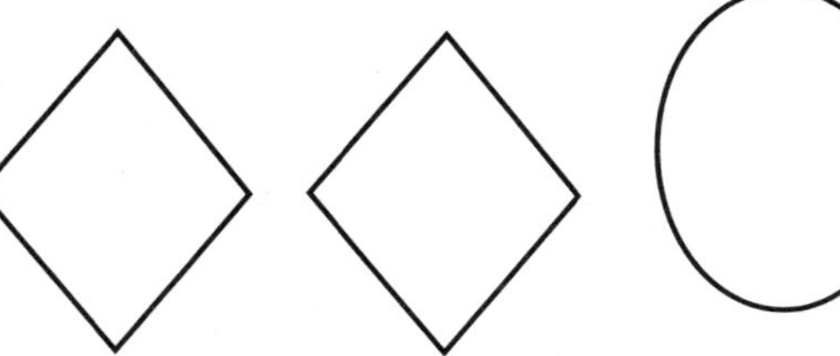 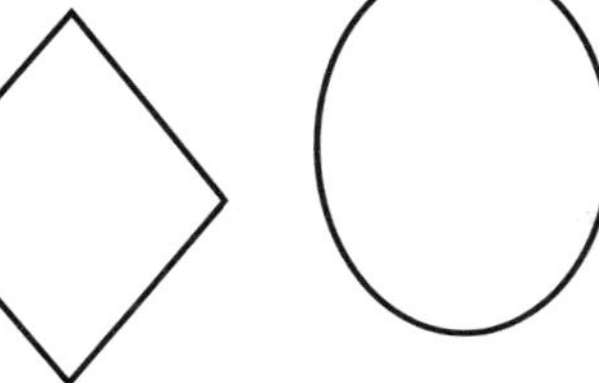 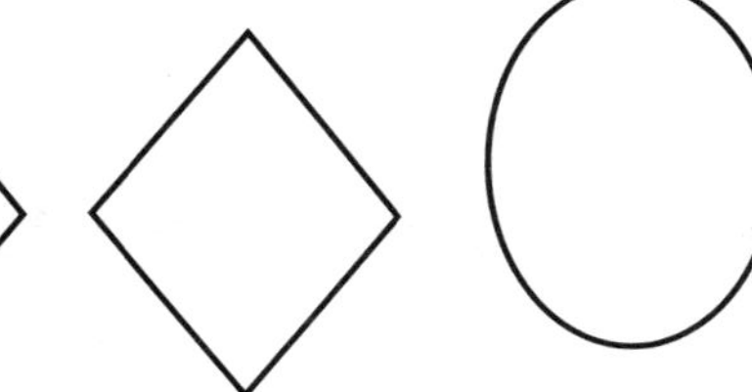 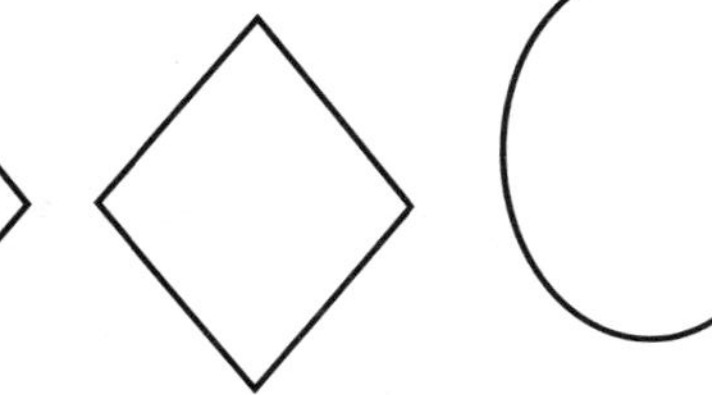 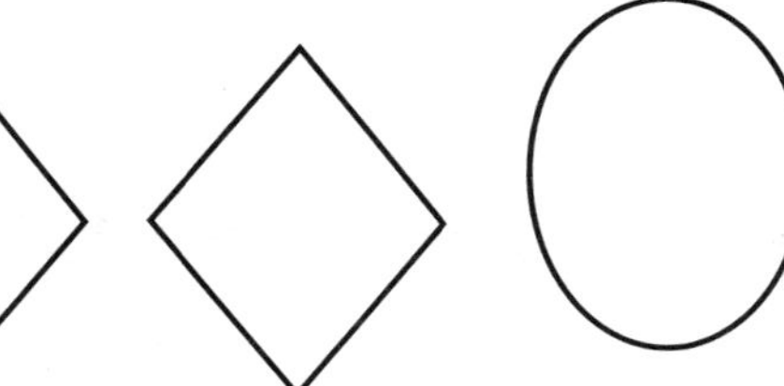 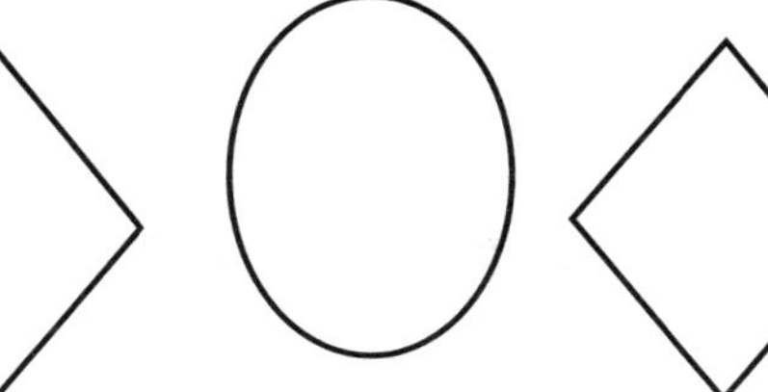 ______ ______ ______

63 Name: ______________________

Shape Patterns: AABB

Draw shapes to complete each pattern.

1. ______ ______ ______ ______

2. ______ ______ ______ ______

3. ______ ______ ______ ______

Name: ______________________

Draw shapes to complete each pattern.

1.    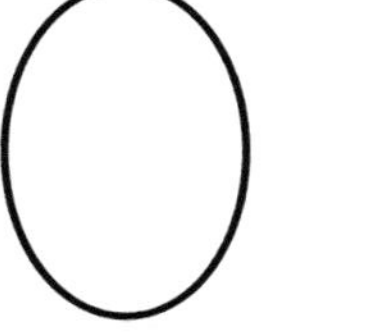 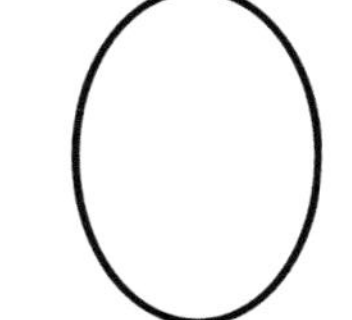  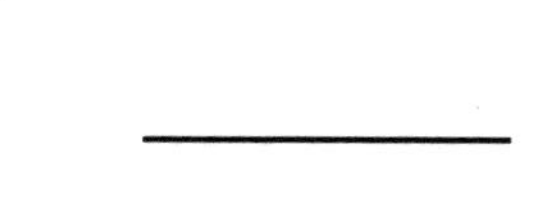 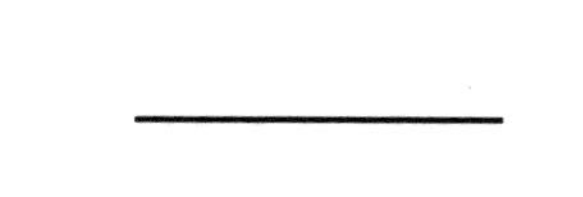 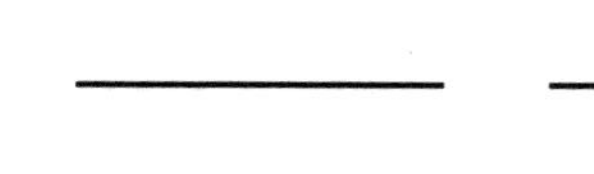 ______ ______ ______ ______

2. 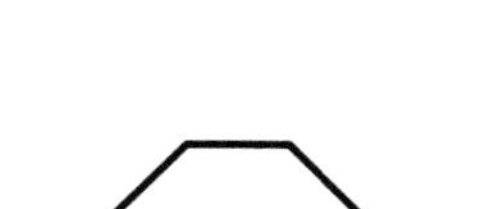 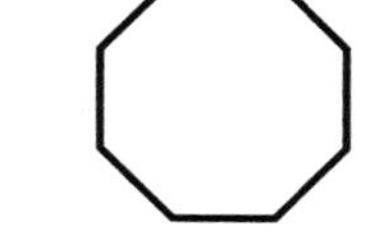 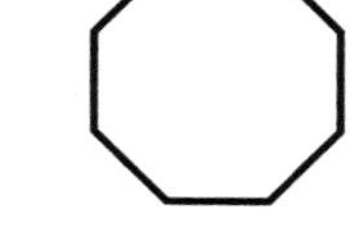 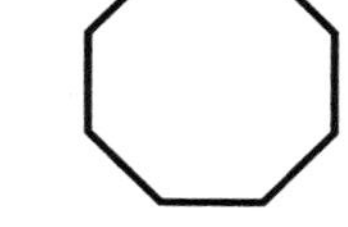 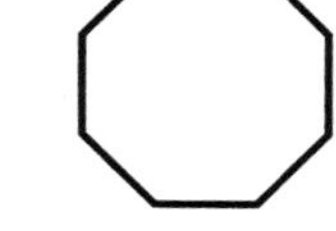 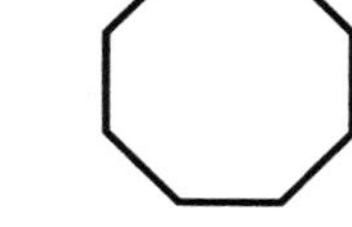 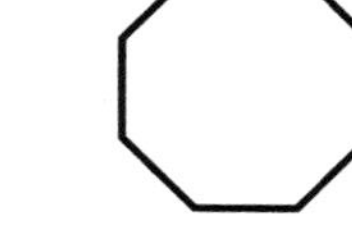 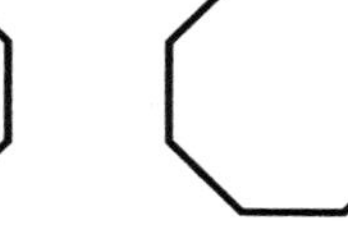 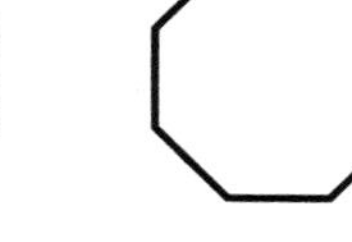 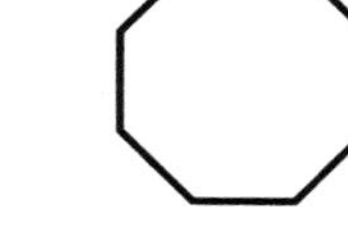 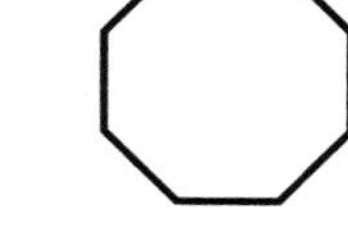 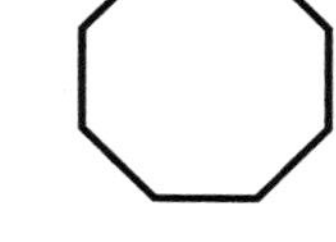 ______ ______ ______ ______

3. 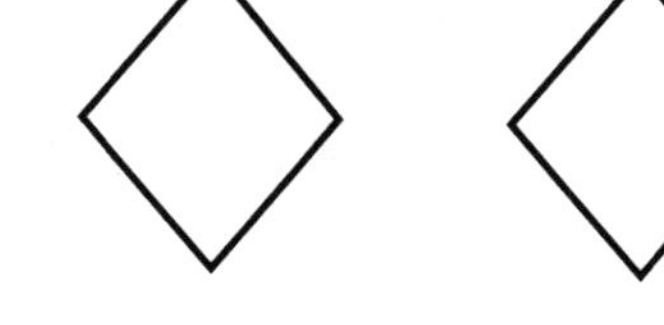 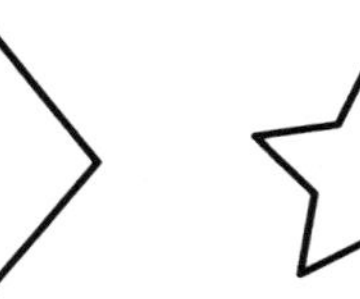    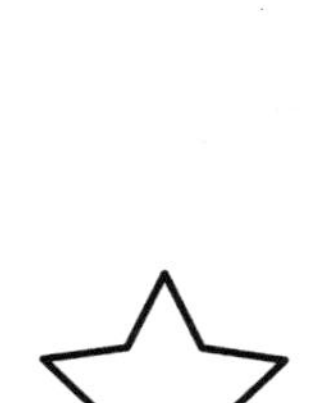    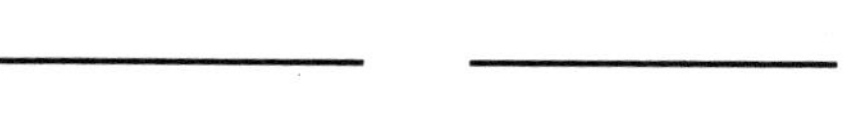 ______ ______ ______ ______

65 Name: ______________________

Shape Patterns: ABC

Draw shapes to complete each pattern.

1. ______ ______ ______

2. ______ ______ ______

3. ______ ______ ______

Name: ______________________

Draw shapes to complete each pattern.

1. 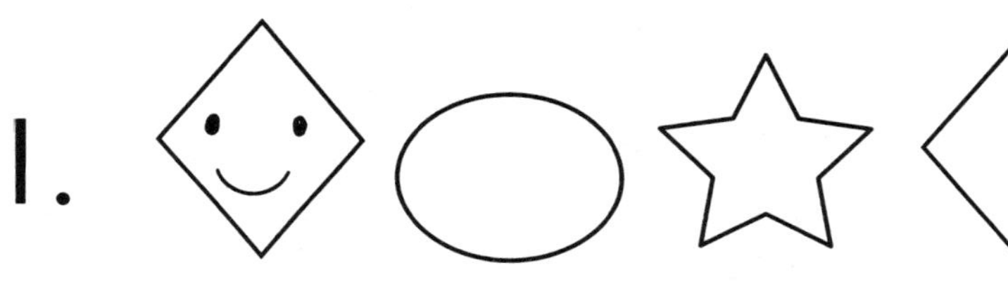 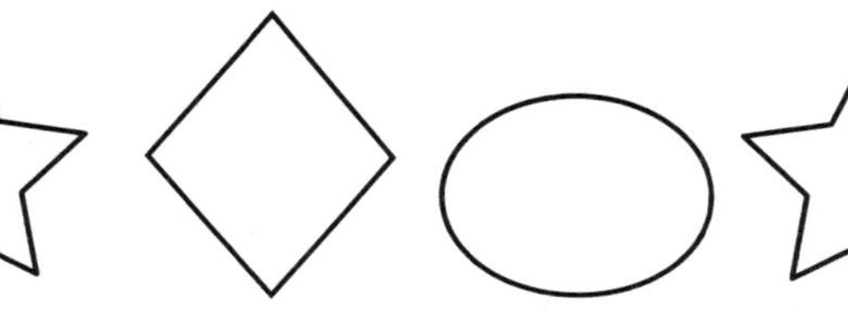 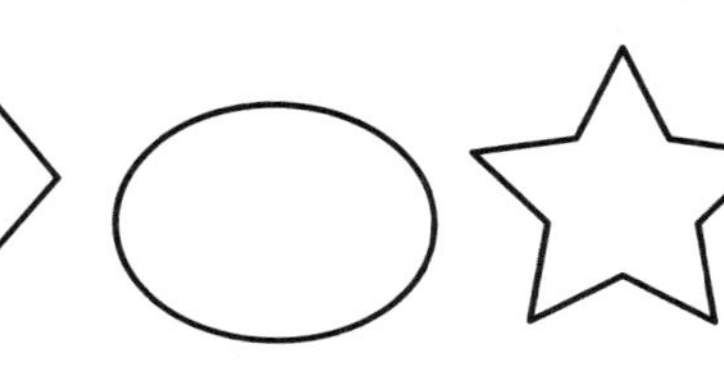 ______ ______ ______

2. 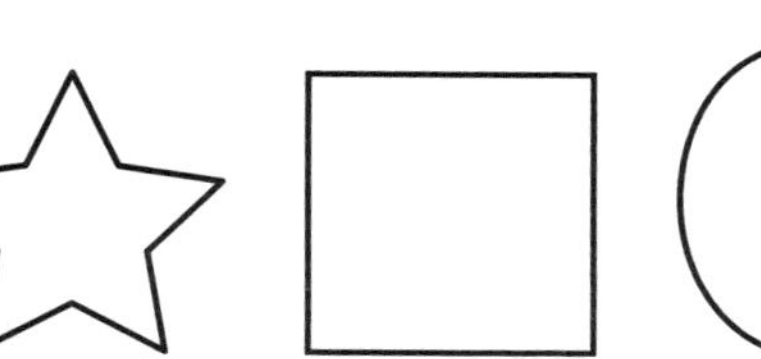 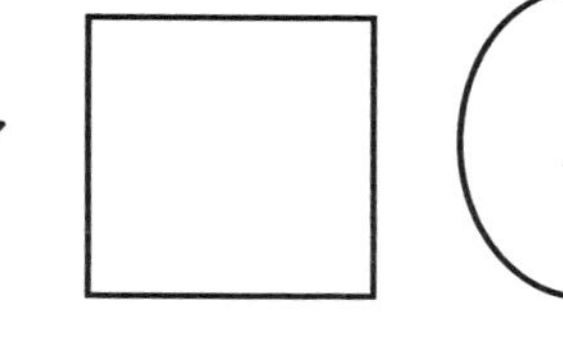 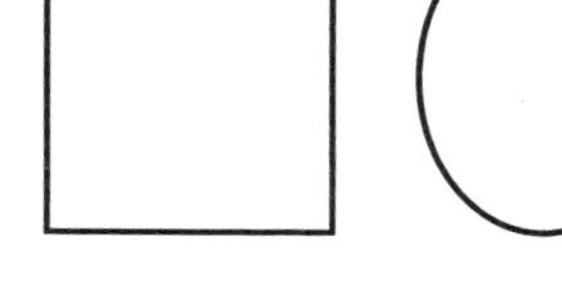 ______ ______ ______

3.   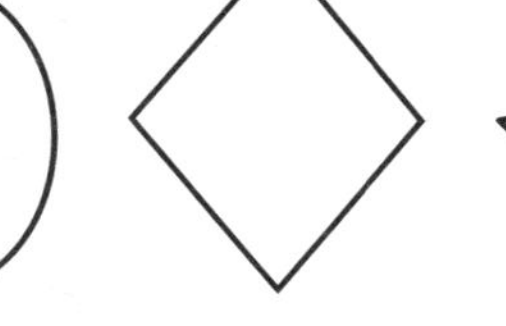   ______ ______ ______

67 Name: ____________________

Color each shape.
Draw an x on the
blue △.

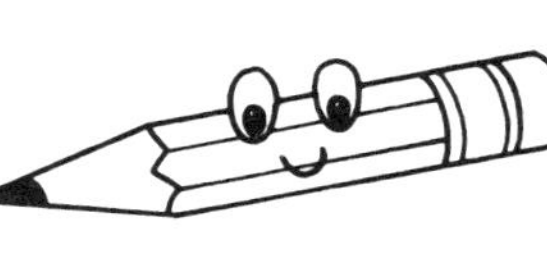

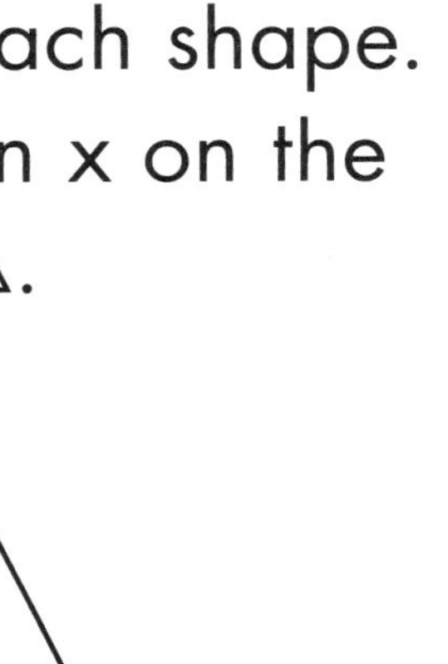

blue

yellow

red

green

Color each shape.
Draw an x on the
red ○.

orange

purple

red

black

Name: ____________________

Color each shape.
Draw an x on the
orange □.

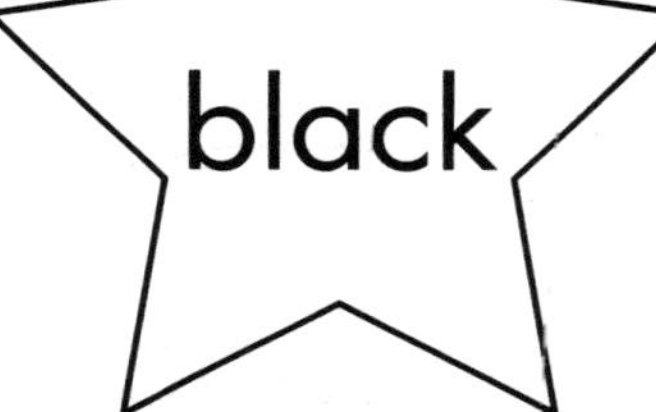

brown

green

blue

orange

Color each shape.
Draw an x on the
green ☆.

blue

black

green

red

Name: ____________________

Color each shape.
Draw an x on the
small blue △.

blue

red

red

blue

Color each shape.
Draw an x on the
big red ○.

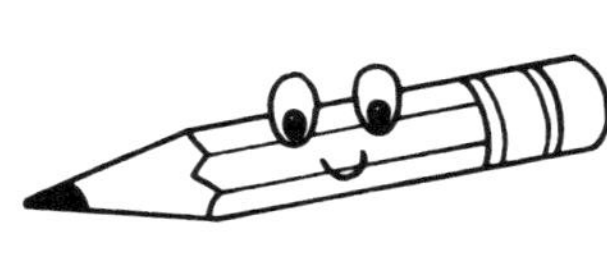

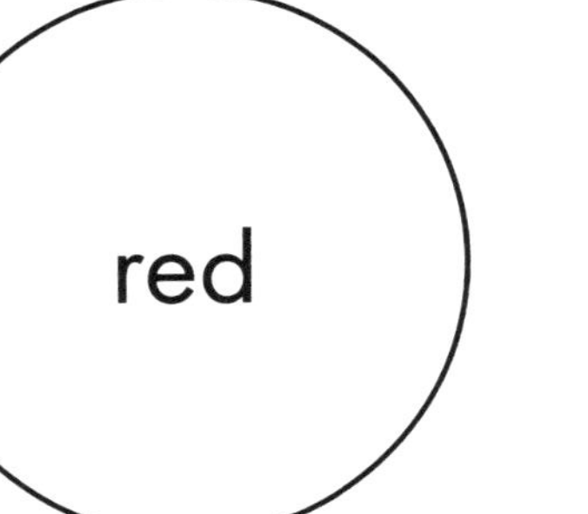

red

Name: ______________________

Color each shape.
Draw an x on the
big orange □.

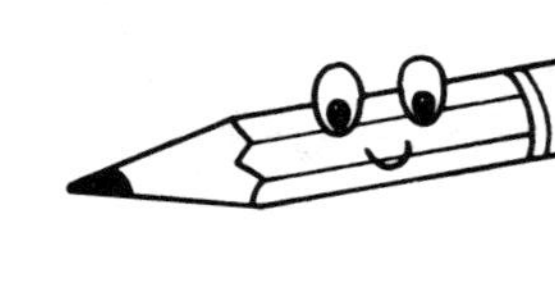

yellow

orange

yellow

orange

Color each shape.
Draw an x on the
small blue ☆.

red

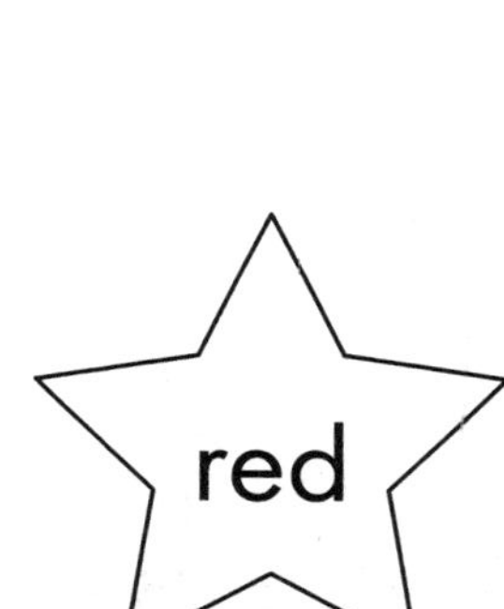

red

blue

blue

Name: ____________________

Color each shape brown.
Draw an x on the
small ◇.

Color each shape red.
Draw an x on the
big ☆.

72

Name: ______________________

Color each shape green.
Draw an x on the
big ⬡.

Color each shape purple.
Draw an x on the
small ▭.

73 Name: ____________________

Draw pictures to complete each pattern.

1.        ________ ________

2.      ________ ________

3.       ________ ________

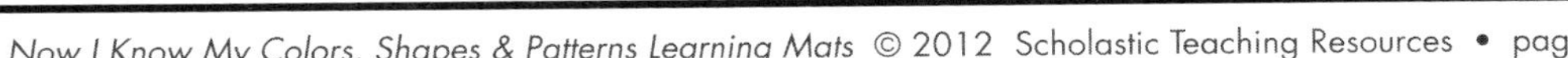

Name: ______________________

Draw pictures to complete each pattern.

1.           ________ ________

2.    ________ ________

3.          ________ ________

Name: ____________________

Draw pictures to complete each pattern.

1.  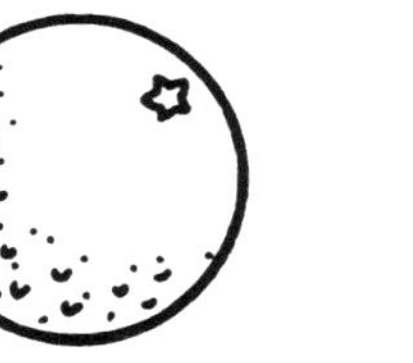 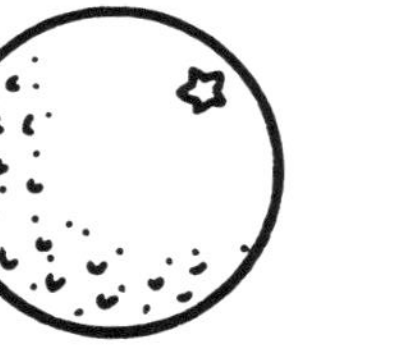      ________ ________

2.    ________ ________

3.     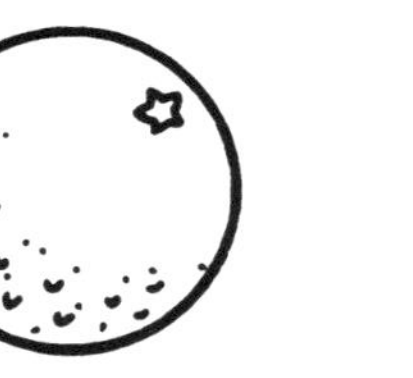  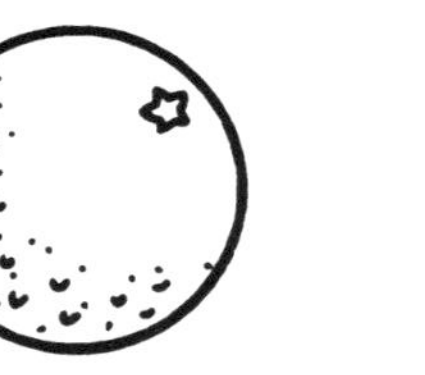 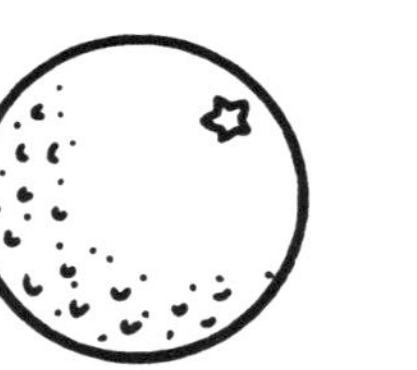 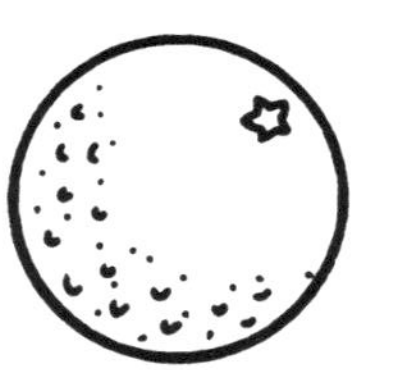 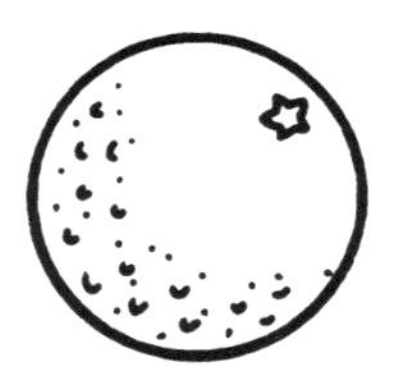 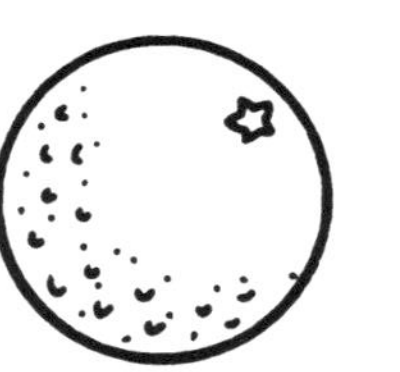 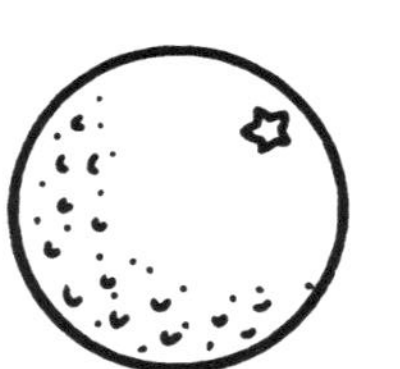 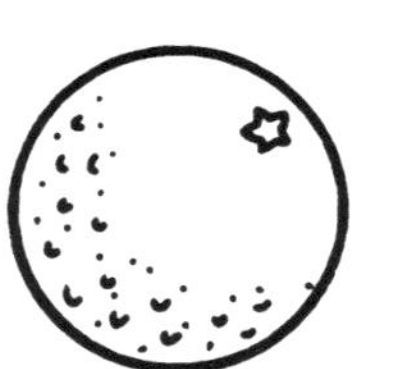 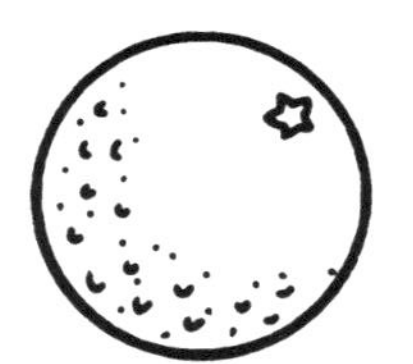 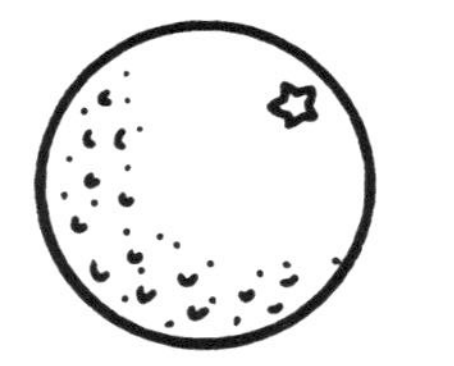 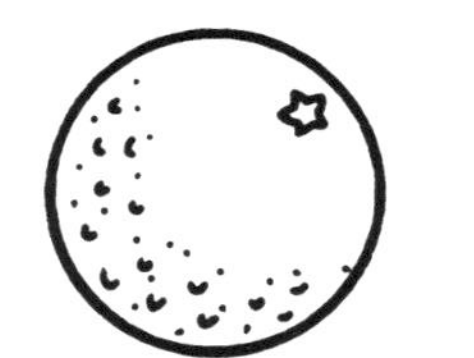 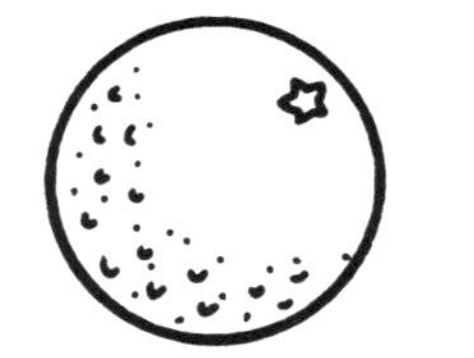 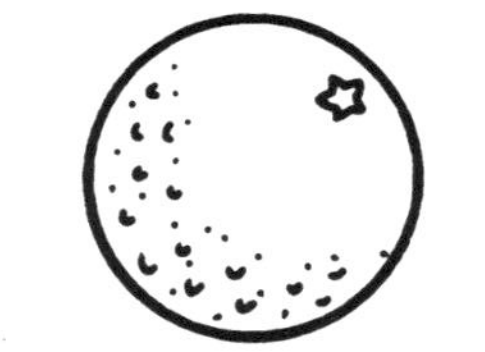 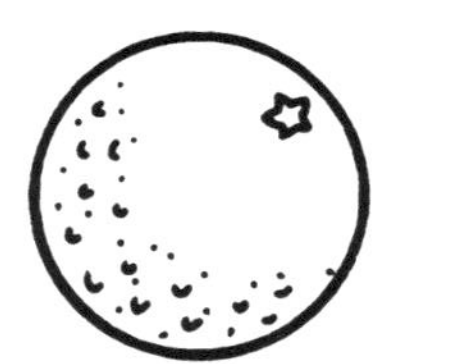 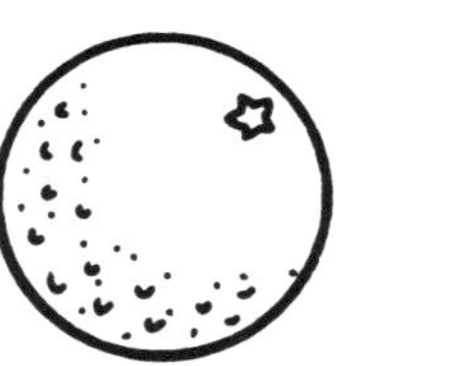 ________ ________

Name: ______________________

Draw pictures to complete each pattern.

1.     ______ ______ ______ ______

2.    ______ ______ ______

3.    ______ ______

Name: ______________________

Write letters to complete each pattern.

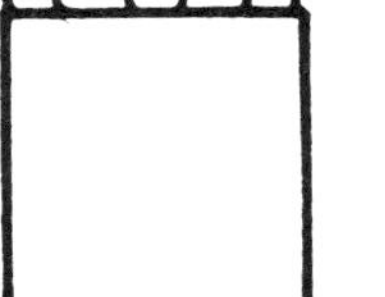

1. D E D E D E ___ ___

2. H I H I ___ ___ ___ ___

3. L M L M ___ ___ ___ ___

Name: ____________________

Write letters to complete each pattern.

1. 

2. 

3. 

Write letters to complete each pattern.

1.

2.
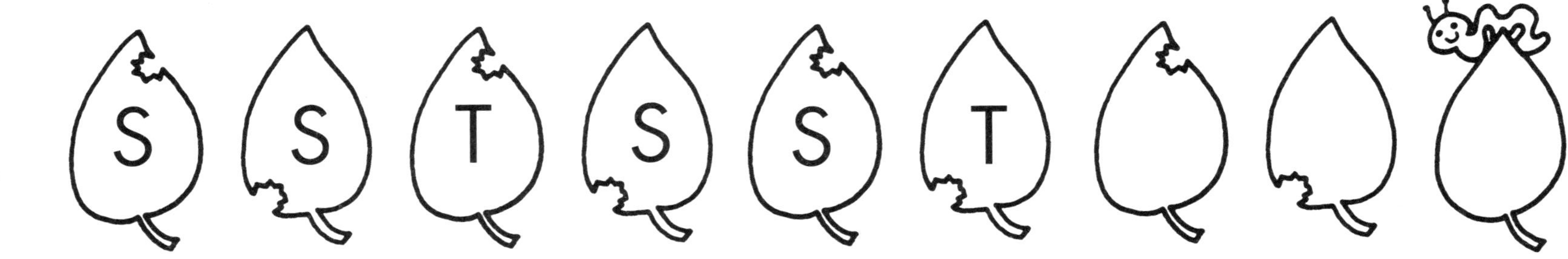

3.

Name: ______________________________

Write letters to complete each pattern.

1.

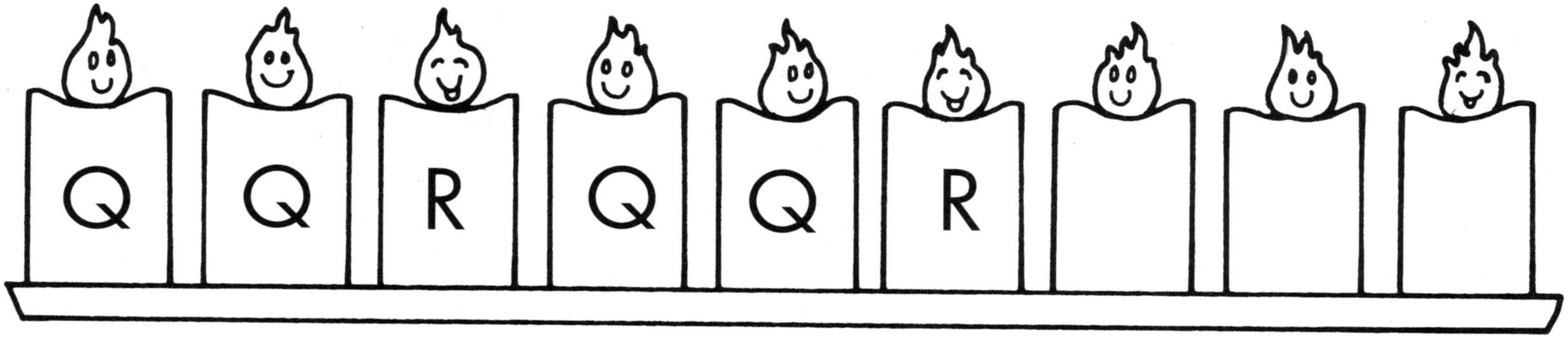

2.

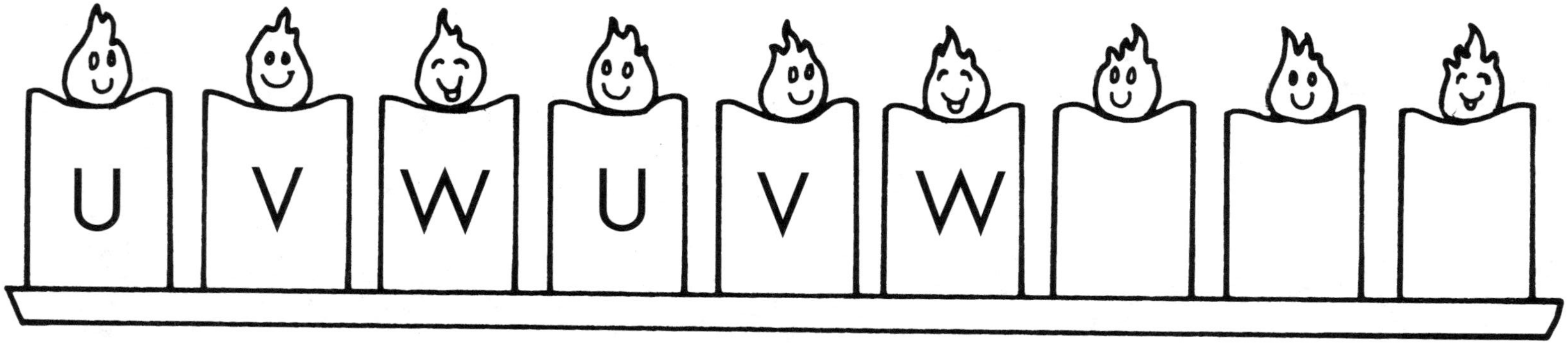

3.

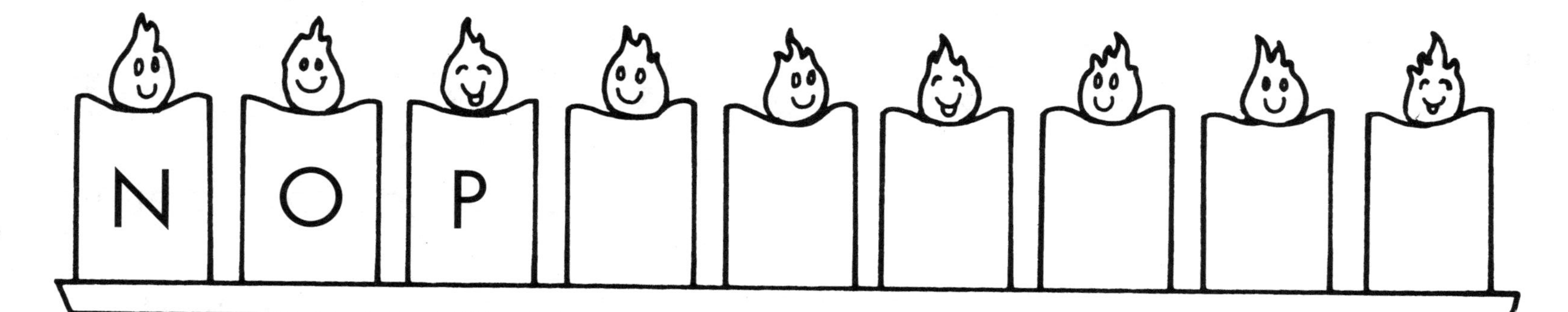

Name: ______________________

Write letters to complete each pattern.

Name: ______________________

Write letters to complete each pattern.

1. 

2. 

3. 

Name: ____________________

Write letters to complete each pattern.

1. 2.

3.

Name: ____________________

Write letters to complete each pattern.

 Name: ____________________

Write letters to complete each pattern.

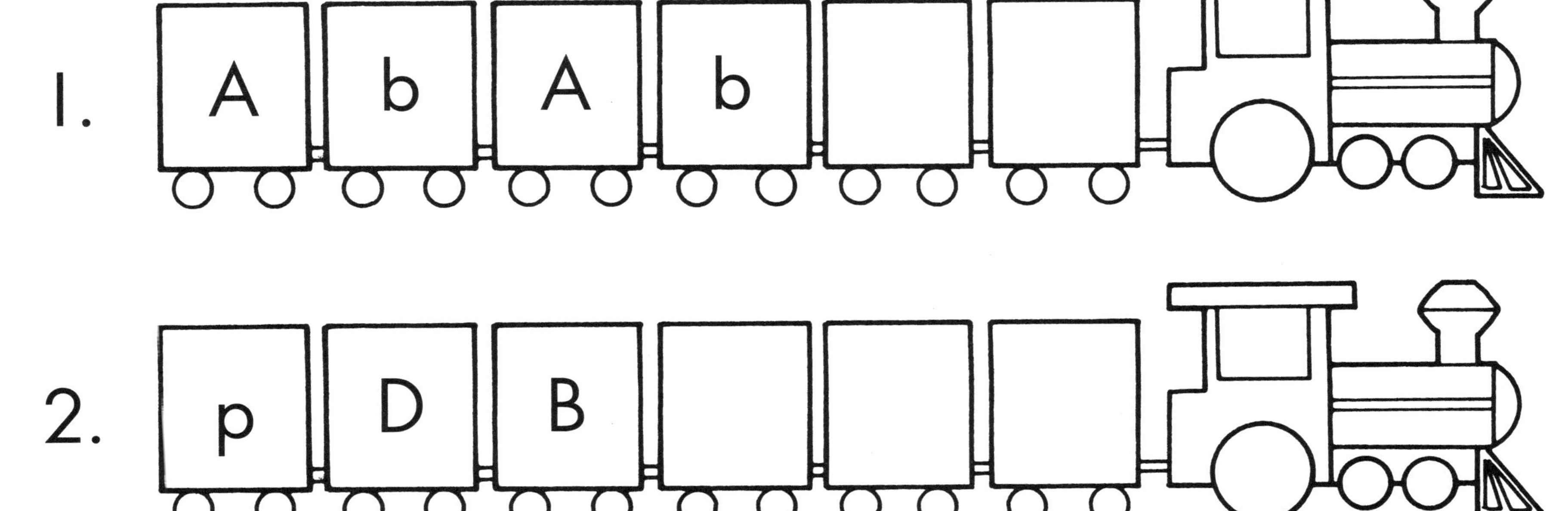

Name: ____________________

Write letters to complete each pattern.

1.

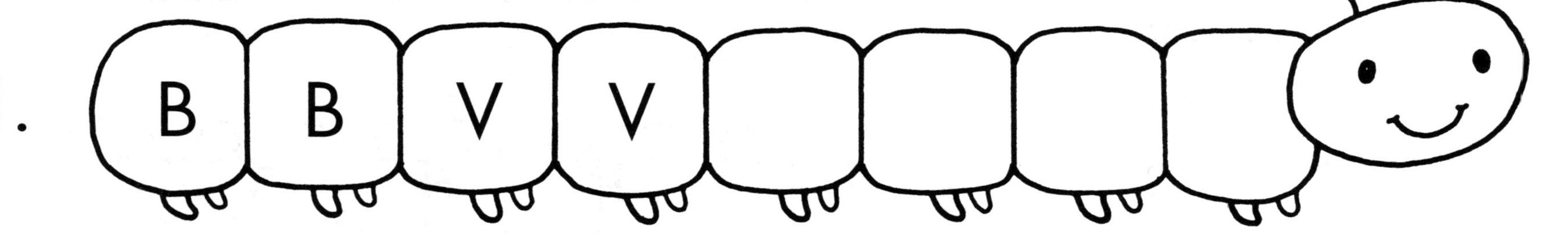

2.

3.

Name: ______________________

Write numbers to complete each pattern.

Name: ______________________

Write numbers to complete each pattern.

1. 1 3 1 3 ___ ___ ___ ___

2. 2 2 4 4 ___ ___ ___ ___

3. 3 3 5 5 ___ ___ ___ ___

Write numbers to complete each pattern.

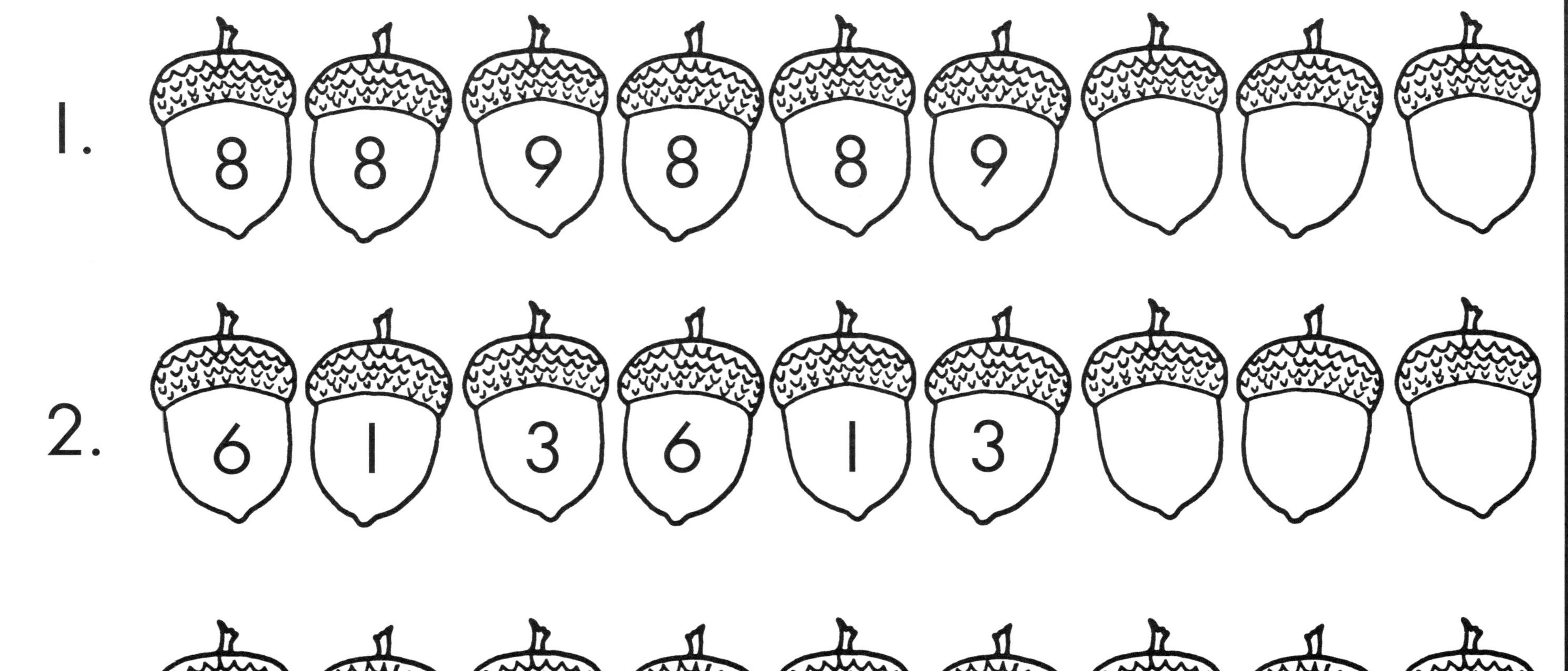

Name: ____________________

Write numbers to complete each pattern.

1.
2.
3.

91 Name: ____________________ Patterns: Review

Complete each pattern.

1. 2 A B 2 A B ___ ___ ___

2. 

3. 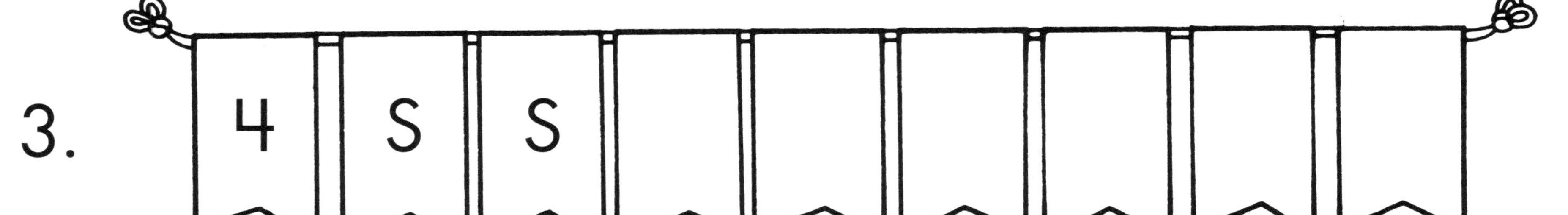

Name: ______________________

Complete each pattern.

1. 8 8 M 8 8 M

2.

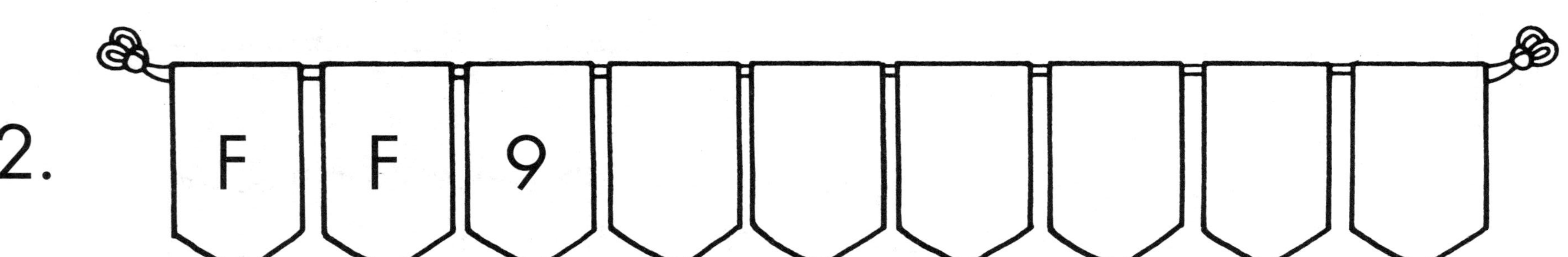

3.

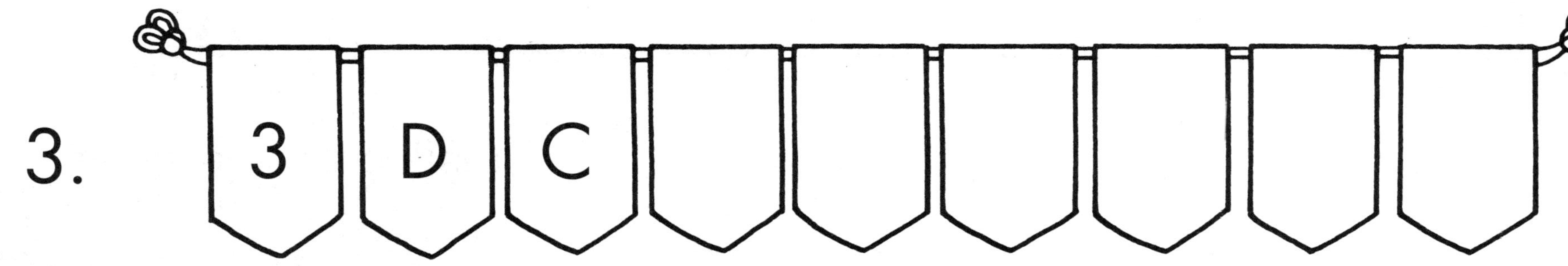

93 Name: ____________________

What comes next in each pattern? Circle your answer.

1.

2.

3.

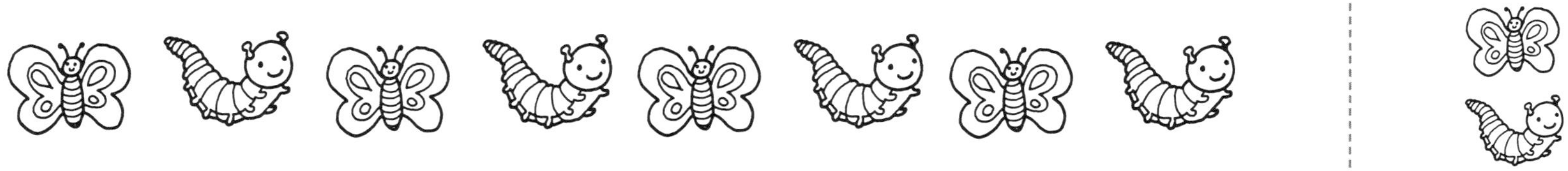

Draw your own pattern! Use two pictures.

______ ______ ______ ______ ______ ______

Name: ______________________________

What comes next in each pattern? Circle your answer.

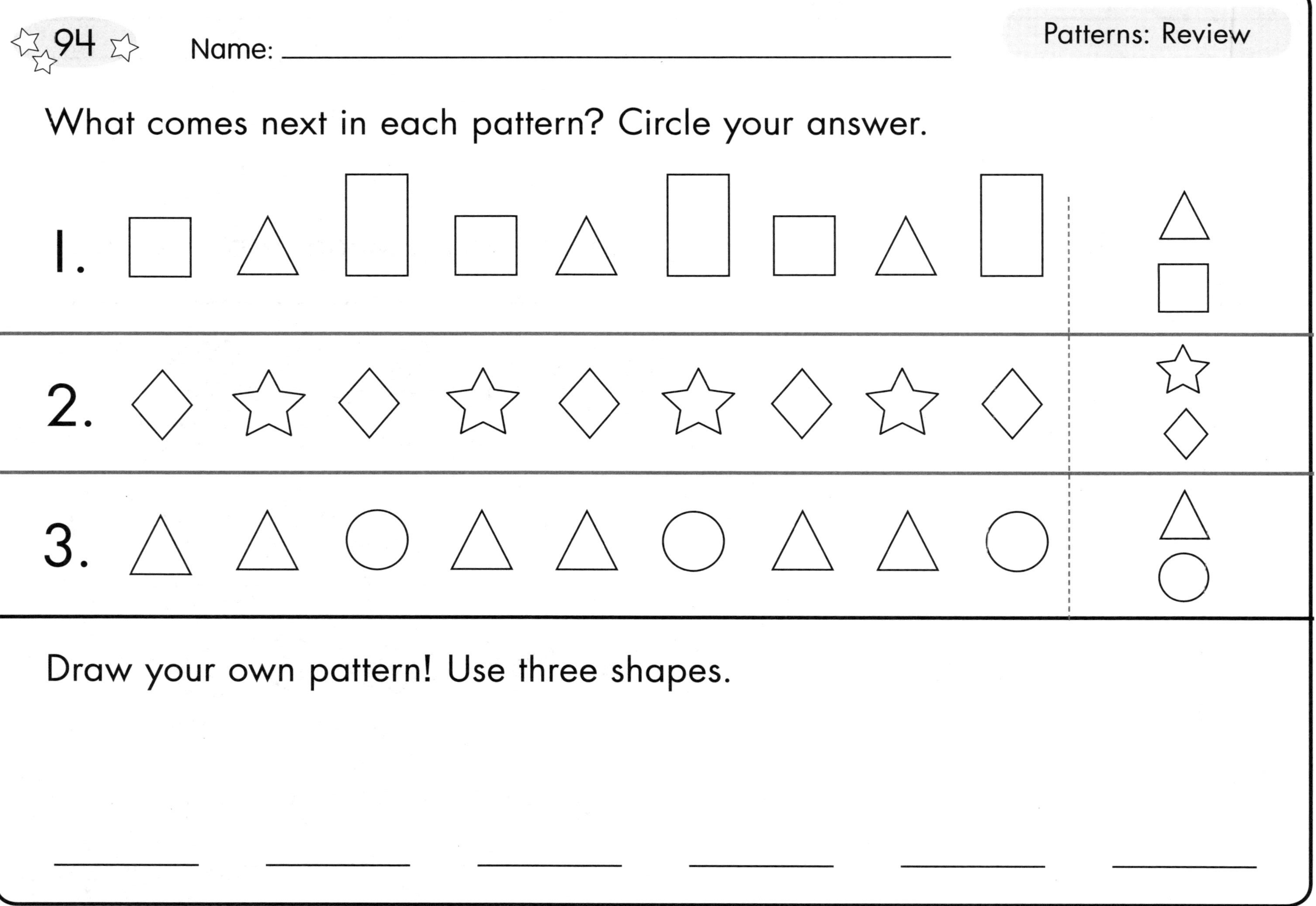

1.

2.

3.

Draw your own pattern! Use three shapes.

_____ _____ _____ _____ _____ _____

Name: ____________________

Finish labeling each pattern.

1. A B A B A B ___ ___

2. A B A B ___ ___ ___ ___

Draw your own **AB** pattern. Use pictures.

___ ___ ___ ___ ___ ___
A B A B A B

Name: ____________________

Finish labeling each pattern.

1. A B A B ___ ___ ___ ___

2. A B ___ ___ ___ ___ ___ ___

Draw your own **AB** pattern. Label the pattern.

___ ___ ___ ___ ___ ___

Name: ____________________

Finish labeling each pattern.

1. A A B A A B ___ ___ ___

2. A A B ___ ___ ___ ___ ___ ___

Draw your own **AAB** pattern. Use pictures.

___ ___ ___ ___ ___ ___

A A B A A B

Name: ____________________

Finish labeling each pattern.

  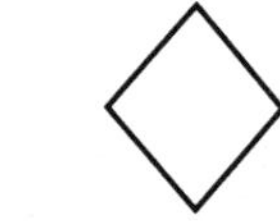 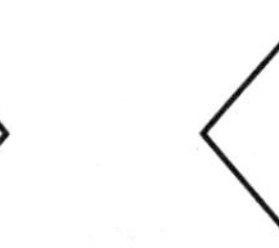  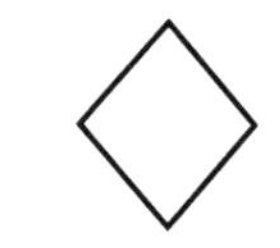 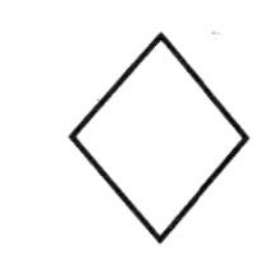 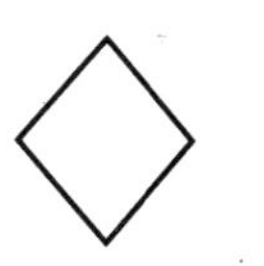 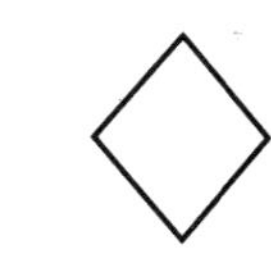 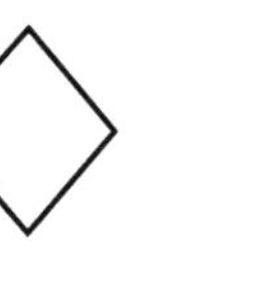 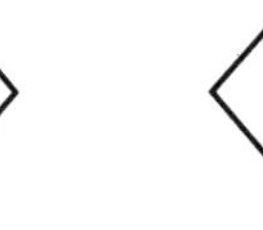 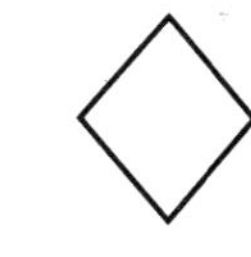 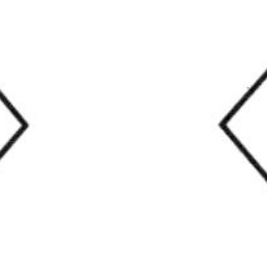 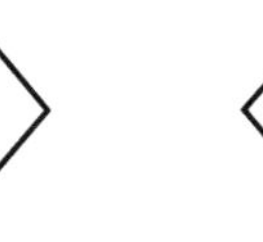 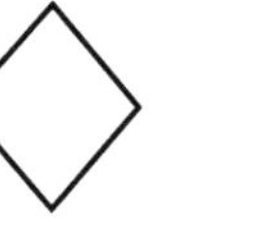              

1. A A B A ___ ___ ___ ___ ___

            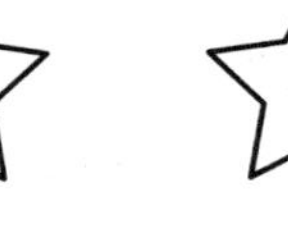  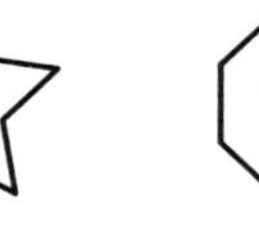 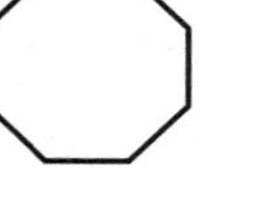      

2. A A B ___ ___ ___ ___ ___ ___

Draw your own **AAB** pattern. Label the pattern.

 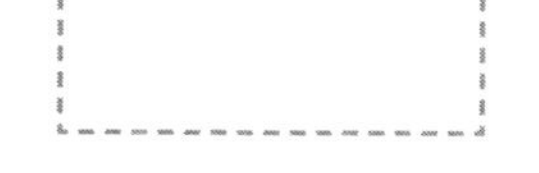 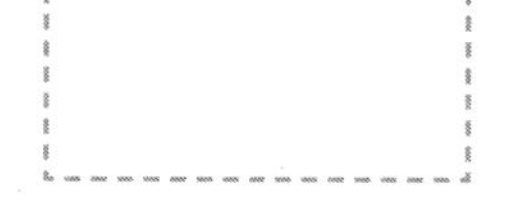

___ ___ ___ ___ ___ ___

99 Name: ____________________ Identifying Patterns

Finish labeling each pattern.

1. A B B A B B ___ ___ ___

2. A B B ___ ___ ___ ___ ___ ___

Draw your own **ABB** pattern. Use pictures.

___ ___ ___ ___ ___ ___

A B B A B B

100 Name: ____________________

Finish labeling each pattern.

1. A B B A ___ ___ ___ ___ ___

2. A B B ___ ___ ___ ___ ___ ___

Draw your own **ABB** pattern. Label the pattern.

___ ___ ___ ___ ___ ___

Name: ____________________

Finish labeling each pattern.

1. A A B B A A ____ ____

2. A A B B ____ ____ ____ ____

Draw your own **AABB** pattern. Use pictures.

____ ____ ____ ____ ____ ____ ____ ____

A A B B A A B B

102 Name: ____________________

Identifying Patterns

Finish labeling each pattern.

1. A A B ___ ___ ___ ___ ___

2. A A ___ ___ ___ ___ ___ ___

Draw your own **AABB** pattern. Label the pattern.

___ ___ ___ ___ ___ ___ ___ ___

Name: ____________________

Finish labeling each pattern.

 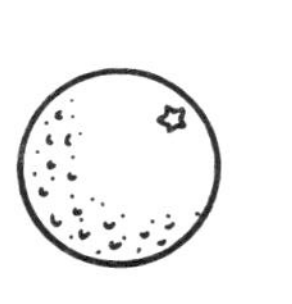    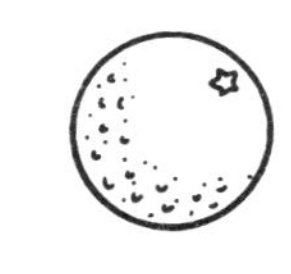   

1. A B C A B C ___ ___ ___

  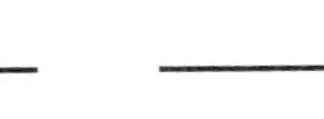   

2. A B C ___ ___ ___ ___ ___ ___

Draw your own **ABC** pattern. Use pictures.

___ ___ ___ ___ ___ ___

A B C A B C

Name: ____________________

Finish labeling each pattern.

   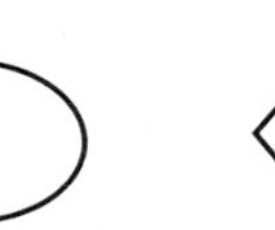   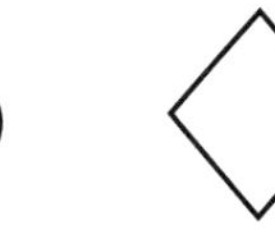 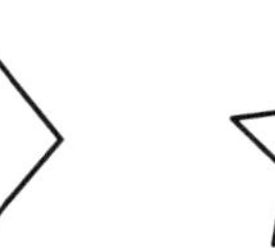 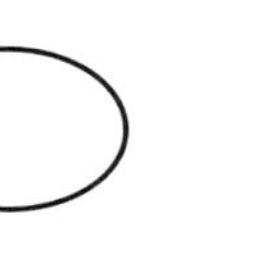 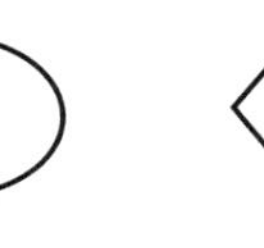 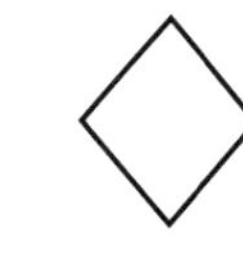 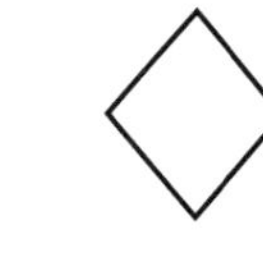 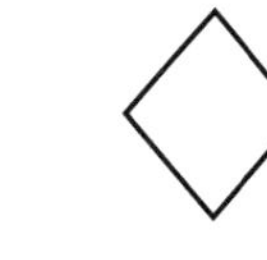 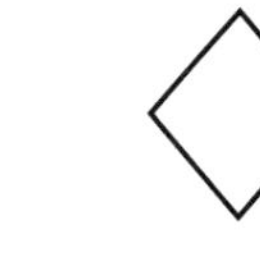 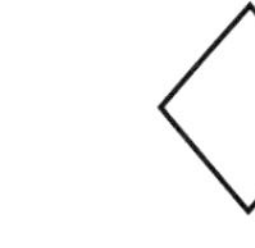 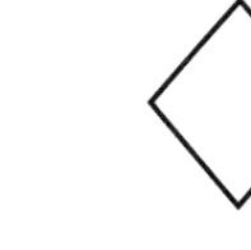  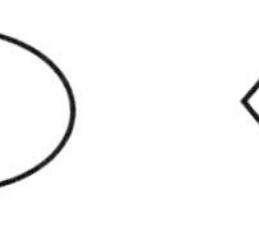 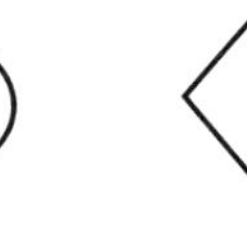 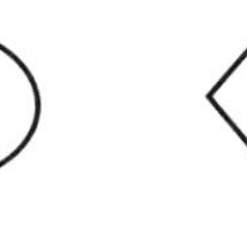 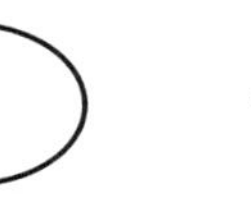 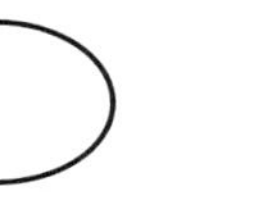 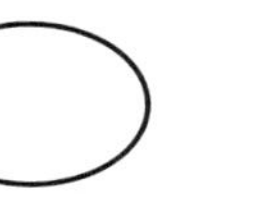 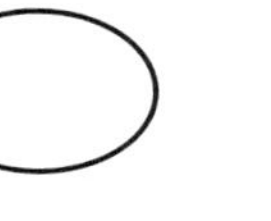    

1. A B C A ___ ___ ___ ___ ___

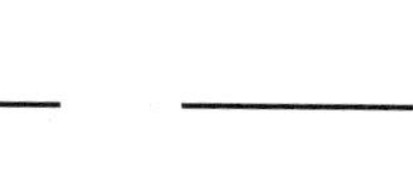 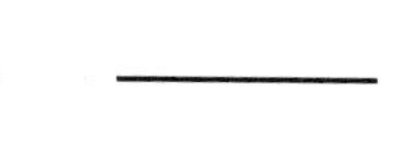 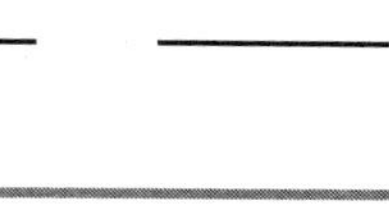 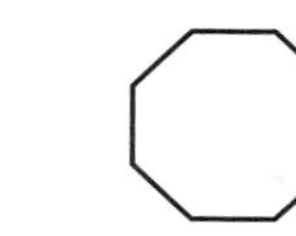 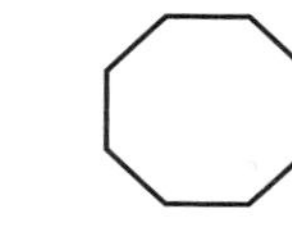   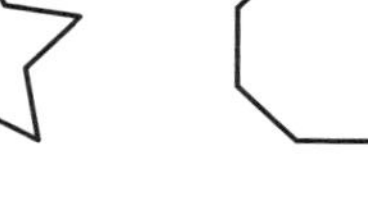 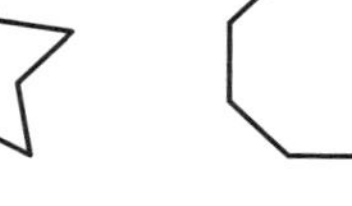 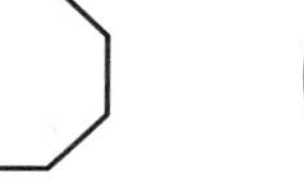      

2. A B C ___ ___ ___ ___ ___ ___

Draw your own **ABC** pattern. Label the pattern.

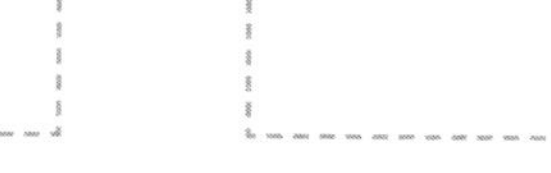 

___ ___ ___ ___ ___ ___